Spencer's
ILLUSTRATED
COMPUTER
DICTIONARY

Spencer's
ILLUSTRATED
COMPUTER
DICTIONARY

Donald D. Spencer, Ph.D.

250 Illustrations

CAMELOT PUBLISHING COMPANY
Ormond Beach, Florida

Printed in the United States of America

Printed on acid-free paper

TRADEMARKS
Trademarked names appear throughout this dictionary. Rather than list the names and entities that own the trademarks or insert a trademark symbol with each mention of the trademarked name, the publisher states that it is using the names only for editorial purposes and to the benefit of the trademark owner with no intention of infringing upon that trademark.

Library of Congress Cataloging-in-Publication Data

Spencer, Donald D.
    Spencer's illustrated computer dictionary / Donald D. Spencer.
        p.   cm.
    Previous eds. published unter title: The illustrated computer
dictionary.
    ISBN 0-89218-220-2
    1. Computers--Dictionaries. I. Spencer, Donald D. Illustrated
computer dictionary. II. Title.
    QA76. 15.S67 1995
    004' .03--dc20
                          94-33107
                              CIP

Published by
CAMELOT PUBLISHING COMPANY
P.O. Box 1357
Ormond Beach, FL 32175

To my son
Michael
(1971 - 1992)
who used computers
most of his life.

PREFACE

It is unlikely that any field has contributed more new terms (or new meanings of old ones) to the language in the last few years than has computer technology. This is largely because computer technology is itself a new and changing field. As it evolves, fresh terminology must be developed to communicate, describe, and define the heretofore unknown concepts, components, and techniques. Compiled by an internationally known computer science educator and author, *Spencer's Illustrated Computer Dictionary* will help even the novice computer user to better understand the language of computers.

This dictionary offers up-to-date coverage of terms used in reference to hardware, software, programming, logic, and computer graphics, a well as those used in ancillary fields such as desktop publishing, computer networks, computer graphics, data communications and artificial intelligence. Areas of frequent application are also covered, particularly mathematics and business administration.

The primary objective of this dictionary is to present compactly and concisely the most common terms used by computer users. Familiarity with the vocabulary of any business or profession is absolutely mandatory if people working in those areas expect to succeed. Lack of knowledge can cause anger, failure, frustration, and loss of time and effort. This book should help computer users overcome many of the problems associated with learning the terminology of an unfamiliar field. This book is intended for several kinds of readers. It is a basic reference book for the person who knows little or nothing about computers but wants to learn. Business people, professionals, students, teachers, and others will find it a useful source book. Computer professionals will find it a handy reference book.

The keynote of this book is clarity — without sacrifice of authority and precision. All definitions are simple and stand as independent units of explanation. Technical terms are kept out of the definitions as much as possible. In a few cases where a special terminology is required, the expressions used are carefully defined, and related terms or concepts are indicated by cross-references.

Spencer's Illustrated Computer Dictionary contains more than 1600 entries involved in using computers. It contains all the terms that most often confuse a beginner. In many cases, definitions are supported by illustrations in order to aid in the clarification of technical points and other explanations beyond the written definitions.

HOW TO USE THIS DICTIONARY

The terms in this dictionary appear in alphabetical order of the complete term (spaces and hyphens don't count); for example, **computerese** comes between **computer crime** and **computer family**. This order contrasts with some dictionaries in which the alphabetical order is based on a heavier weighing of the first word in a term; for example all terms commencing with "computer" precede all terms commencing with "computerization."

All terms listed in the dictionary are in **boldface**. Cross-references that are important to an understanding of any term are given in *italics*.

If you cannot find a word, it might be listed in a slightly different form. For example, you might try looking for "compute" and find the description under "computing." Only one definition has been included to keep from cluttering the book with the obvious.

The terms normally appear in boldface, lower case characters. Proper names and nouns are headed by an upper case letter, for example, **Babbage, Charles**. Acronyms are presented in boldface caps and the proper letters are amplified in the text; for example, **RISC** stands for Reduced Instruction Set Computer.

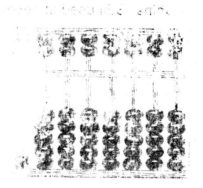

A: A designation for the first floppy disk drive in IBM-compatible microcomputers; B: drive is the second floppy disk drive; C: drive is the hard disk drive.

abacus Ancient device for doing simple calculations that uses movable beads threaded on a grid of wires. First used in ancient Mediterranean cultures and ancient China. Still used in several oriental countries.

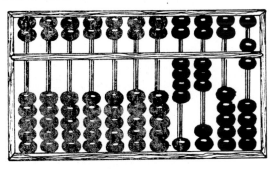

abacus

ABC See *Atanasoff-Berry Computer*.

abort Procedure for terminating a program when a mistake, malfunction, or error occurs.

accelerator A device to speed up either the computer or monitor. Typically a circuit card with an extra processing chip and/or additional RAM.

access (1) Generally, the obtaining of data. To locate desired data. (2) To store on and retrieve data from a disk.

access time Memory access is how fast a character in memory can be transferred to or from the processor. Disk access is an average of how fast the access arm can position the read/write head over the requested track.

accumulator Register or storage location that temporarily holds the result of an arithmetic or logic operation. Commonly used when a series of calculations are to be totaled.

ACM See *Association for Computing Machinery.*

acoustic coupler A type of modem. It translates computer signals into telephone tones and the reverse. This allows computers to communicate with each other by the telephone network.

acronym A word formed from the first letter (or letters) of each word in a phrase or name (e.g. VDT stands for Visual Display Terminal, IC stands for Integrated Circuit, RAM stands for Random-Access Memory and AI stands for Artificial Intelligence).

activate To put a unit or device into an operational state.

active cell In a spreadsheet, the cell in which the cursor currently is positioned. Information may be entered, altered, or deleted by the user when the cell is active. Also called the *current cell.*

active file File currently being used.

active program Any program that is loaded into computer memory and ready to be executed.

active window When using a graphics user interface, the active window is the window currently in use.

activity light A small light on the computer's front panel that indicates when a disk drive is reading or writing data.

Ada An extremely powerful high-level structured programming language designed by the United States Department of Defense to ensure transportability of programs. Ada was derived from the Pascal language but has major semantic and syntactical extensions. Ada was named after the first programmer Augusta Ada Byron, Countess of Lovelace (1815-1852). It was she who suggested to Charles Babbage (1792-1871), an English mathematician who invented the machine which was the forerunner of the modern computer, several programming principles that remain valid to this day.

adapter (1) Device that allows compatibility between different equipment. (2) Device that changes alternating current to direct current.

12

add-on Component or device added to a computer system to increase its storage capacity, to modify its architecture, or to upgrade its performance.

address Identification — such as a label, number, or name — that designates a particular location in storage or any other data destination or source.

Adobe Illustrator A PostScript-based, Apple Macintosh drawing program with powerful capabilities. A complete set of tools for drawing, blending, grouping and transforming objects that enables users to create very sophisticated graphics. Adobe Illustrator was introduced in 1987 by Adobe Systems Inc.

Adobe Photoshop A powerful and versatile 24-bit image processing program, for the Apple Macintosh computer. It can be used as a paint, pre-press, color correction and darkroom system. Designers can work with scanned photos, slides, electronic artwork or create original graphics using a full range of filters, painting, drawing and selection tools.

Adobe Systems, Inc. Founded in 1982, the company has introduced several powerful software products including the Postscript page image description language for text/graphics systems, Adobe Illustrator and Adobe Photoshop.

Adobe Type Manager A font generator and utility for the Apple Macintosh computer from Adobe Systems Inc.

adventure game A computer game which involves controlling a character through a series of challenges and puzzles.

AFIPS Acronym for American Federation of Information Processing Societies. The U.S. representative of IFIP, founded in 1961, dedicated to advancing information processing in the U.S. It was dissolved in 1990 and replaced with FOCUS (Federation On Computing in the U.S.). See *IFIP*.

agent A program that can carry out tasks for users, things such as finding data remotely, interpreting and responding to messages, and filtering data for content. An agent, as its name implies, represents a computer users interest to some system (or to other people), which (or who) may also have agents representing them. What would it be like to have a software agent representing you? Imagine that when you dial a long-distance telephone number, a software agent in your telephone broadcasts a request for bids. Immediately, software agents for AT&T, MCI, and Sprint place bids based on currently available lines. Your agent awards the call to the lowest bidding company, and the whole operation takes place in an imperceptibly brief time. Not only do you get the lowest possible rate all the time but also billion-dollar companies are bidding for your business as if you were the federal government. It would be like that.

AI An acronym for Artificial Intelligence, the study of how to make computer systems behave more as if they were bright and helpful humans.

Aiken, Howard Hathaway (1900-1973) Headed the team of people who designed and built one of the first electromechanical computers, the Automatic Sequence Controlled Calculator (ASCC), at Harvard University, between 1937 and 1944. The ASCC, also called the Mark 1, was made of 765,000 parts, weighed five tons and was 51 feet long. He held many honory degrees from many universities. He was named an IEEE Fellow in 1960 for his contributions to the development of computer science and technology. See *Automatic Sequence Controlled Calculator.*

Howard Aiken

Aldus Corporation A software company that produces products such as PageMaker, one of the pioneer programs for desktop publishing page layout.

Aldus PageMaker A desktop publishing program for IBM-compatible and Apple Macintosh microcomputers. It was introduced in 1985 by Aldus Corporation. This program set the standard for desktop publishing. Paul Brainerd, president of Aldus, coined the term desktop publishing.

algorithm Prescribed set of well-defined, unambiguous rules or processes for the solution of a problem in a finite number of steps. Commonly used as integral parts of computer programs. Thus the study of computers and the study of algorithms are closely related subjects.

aliasing A stepped edge or "staircase" in computer generated images. Appears along lines that are not perfectly horizontal or vertical. Aliasing is especially noticeable in low-resolution monitors.

alignment Adjustment of tolerances within the mechanism of a device so it will operate properly.

Allen, Paul G. Cofounder of Microsoft Corporation (with William Gates) in 1975. He and Gates wrote the first BASIC interpreter for the Intel 8080 microprocessor which was used in the Altair 8800 microcomputer. Versions of Microsoft BASIC were licensed to the IBM Corporation, Apple Computer, Tandy Corporation, and many other hardware vendors. Microsoft Corporation continued to develop a wide variety of software products. Allen left Microsoft and founded his own software company called Asymetyrix Corporation. See *Gates, William* and *Microsoft Corporation.*

Paul Allen

alphanumeric data Data represented by digits, letters and special characters.

alpha test The product test stage during the research and development of a new product during which the first manufactured version of a system is tested with application software. The preliminary testing stage of software development. See *beta test.*

Altair 8800 The first microcomputer system to achieve some degree of commercial success. It was introduced in kit form in 1974 by Micro Instrumentation and Telemetry Systems (MITS). It sold for $400 and was the first commercially successful microcomputer.

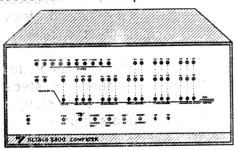

Altair 8800

Alto A personal computer designed by the Xerox Corporation in 1973. This computer pioneered the icon operating system environment and the use of a mouse. The Alto was the progenitor of the Xerox Star and the Apple Macintosh.

ambient conditions Environmental conditions that surround a computer system, such as light, temperature, and humidity.

Amdahl Corporation A computer manufacturer founded in 1970 by Gene Amdahl. Its purpose was to build IBM compatible mainframes with better performance; first mainframe was the 470/V6 computer released in 1975.

Amdahl, Gene Designer of several early IBM computers. Created an architectural revolution in designing the IBM System/360 computer series in 1964, the first computer to use integrated circuits. An early promoter of the concept of hardware compatibility, he later designed several computers for the Amdahl Corporation. In 1980, he formed Trilogy Corp., an unsuccessful attempt to advance mainframe logic technology, through wafer-scale integration. He now heads up Andor International Ltd., a manufacturer of products for IBM mainframe installations.

Gene Amdahl

American Federation of Information Processing Societies See *AFIPS*.

American National Standards Institute (ANSI) An association formed by industry and the U.S. Government to produce and disseminate computer and computer graphics standards that are acceptable to and used by a majority of companies and the government.

America OnLine (AOL) An online information service with a direct Internet connection. Through AOL you can read from and post to newsgroups, subscribe to mailing lists, access Gopher and search the World-Wide Web. See *Gopher, Internet* and *World-Wide Web*.

Amiga Brand name for a family of microcomputers manufactured by Commodore Business Machines, Inc. The Amiga computers have been used extensively in the areas of computer graphics and animation. The Amiga personal computers are based on the Motorola 68000 microprocessor family. Commodore introduced the Amiga in 1985 and stopped manufacturing the computer in 1994.

analog computer Computer that measures continuously changing conditions, such as temperature and pressure and converts them into quantities. Contrast with *digital computer*.

analysis (1) The investigation of a problem by a consistent, systematic procedure. (2) In program and systems development, the process of studying a problem area to determine what should be done.

16

analyst Person skilled in the definition and development of techniques for solving a problem, especially those techniques for solutions on a computer.

Analytical Engine A device conceived by Charles Babbage in 1833 to perform computations. This machine is considered the forerunner of today's modern electronic computer. See *Babbage, Charles* .

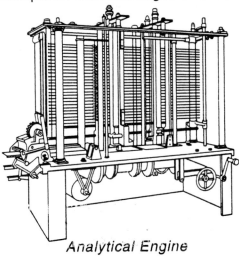

Analytical Engine

analytical graphics Traditional line graphs, pie charts, and bar charts used to illustrate and analyze data. A type of presentation graphics built into a spreadsheet, database, or word processing program.

animation Process of making an object appear to move by rapidly displaying a series of pictures of it, each one in a slightly different position. Technique used for producing computer-generated movies. See *computer animation*.

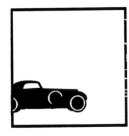

animation

ANSI See *American National Standards Institute*.

antialiasing At low resolutions, diagonal lines in digitized images appear as stair-steps and are called "jaggies." This effect is called "aliasing." Antialiasing is the smoothing or removal of these "jaggies" to recreate smoother diagonal lines.

17

antivirus program A program designed to counter the effects of a virus program.

API See *application program interface*.

APL Acronym for A Programming Language, a mathematically structured programming language. The power of the language is demonstrated by its extended single operators that allow a user to perform directly such calculations as taking the inverse of a matrix or solving a set of linear equations. APL was developed by Kenneth Iverson in the mid-1960s and originally designed for use on IBM mainframes. APL is a very compact, hard to read, scientific programming language. It is used on a wide variety of computers from microcomputers to supercomputers.

append Add on; such as to add new records to a database or to add to the end of a character string or list.

Apple Computer, Inc. One of the first and certainly the most influential of the microcomputer manufacturers. Founded in 1976 by Steven P. Jobs and Stephen G. Wozniak, using the family garage as a base and $100 in capital. Apple made computers that became wildly successful. Because of excellent design principles, the early Apple II family of microcomputers is still useful, and later machines, such as the Macintosh family of microcomputers, have become extremely popular and have greatly affected the design of other machines and of software. The Macintosh computer, with its innovative software, is in a class by itself. Apple Computer, Inc. is a leader in high-performance personal computing. See *Jobs, Steven* and *Wozniak, Stephen*.

Apple key On keyboards produced by Apple Computer, Inc., a special key identified by the Apple logo symbol. The key is used by the operating system and certain applications programs.

AppleLink An Apple Computer Inc. online business service. In 1994 it became part of eWorld, an Apple online computer service.

Apple Macintosh See *Macintosh*.

AppleTalk A network scheme designed primarily for the Apple Macintosh computer. The system often uses the relatively slow LocalTalk hardware, but has grown in popularity because of its low cost, ease of use and installation, and general reliability. It allows computers to share files and peripherals.

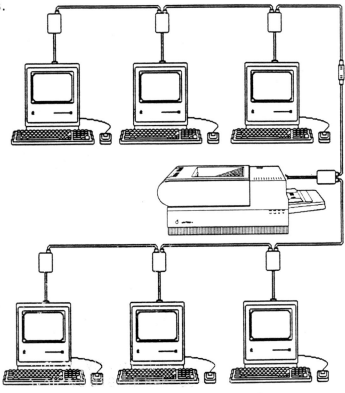

AppleTalk

Apple II A family of personal computers from Apple Computer, Inc. The first Apple II was introduced in 1977. The computer family now includes several models widely used in secondary schools, businesses and homes. The Apple II computers are based on the MOS Technology 6502 microprocessor. This family of Apple microcomputers help pioneer the microcomputer revolution.

Apple II

19

AppleWorks An integrated software package that runs on the Apple II family of microcomputers. The program combines word processing, spreadsheet, and database management. It was introduced in 1983 by Apple Computer, Inc.

application A software program specially designed for particular user needs or the specific use of a software program. Graphics applications are usually designed to enable the user to manipulate data or images, or to create images from data or from a library of shapes or clip art.

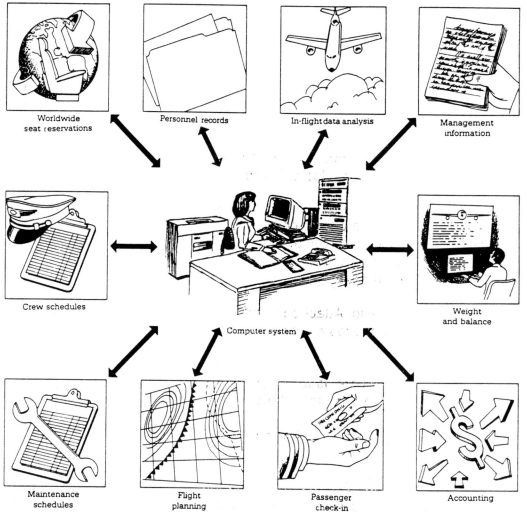

application (airline reservation system)

application program interface (AP!) A set of operating system functions that an application program can use to perform tasks such as managing files and displaying information on the computer display screen.

application programmer Computer programmer who develops applications programs.

application software Software that is specific to the solution of an application problem. Some examples are word processing programs, electronic spreadsheets, games, educational programs, drawing programs, etc.

arcade game Computer video games popularized by coin-operated machines, characterized by high-resolution color graphics, high-speed animation, and sound. Players often use joysticks to control a screen object, and the computer scores points based on the game's rules.

archie A database service that indexes and catalogs files on Internet host computers. Archie enables you to locate a specific file stored on computers around the Internet.

architecture (1) Physical structure of a computer's internal operations, including its registers, memory, instruction set, and input/output structure. (2) The special selection, design, and interconnection of the principal components of a system.

archival storage (1) Refers to memory (on magnetic disks, optical disks, or magnetic tape) used to store data outside of the main memory. (2) Saving digital data for future reference. (3) A storage system for information designed to be kept for a long period of time.

ARCNET An acronym for Attached Resource Computer NETwork, a popular local area network that uses a media-access control method that is similar to token-passing.

area chart Area charts are usually a combination of two line charts with the difference between the two highlighted to accentuate that difference.

argument Variable to which either a logical or a numerical value may be assigned.

arithmetic operation Various manipulations of numerical quantities, including the fundamental operations of addition, subtraction, multiplication and division, as well as exponentiation and extraction of roots.

ARPANET Acronym for Advanced Research Projects Agency NETwork, the first packet switching network and the prototype of Internet.

array (1) Series of related items. (2) Ordered arrangement or pattern of items or numbers, such as a determinant, matrix, vector, or table of numbers.

arrow keys Keyboard keys that are used to move the cursor up, down, left or right on the display screen.

artificial intelligence (AI) A group of technologies that attempt to emulate certain aspects of human behavior, such as reasoning and communicating, as well as to mimic biological senses, including seeing and hearing. Specific technologies include expert systems (also called knowledge-based systems), natural language, neural networks, machine translation and speech recognition. AI is the branch of computer science that is concerned with developing computer systems capable of simulating human reasoning and sensation. AI involves using computers and software that, like the human mind, use stored knowledge to make decisions involving judgement or ambiguity. See *robotics*.

artificial reality A computer generated simulation of reality with which users can interact using specialized peripherals such as data gloves and head-mounted computer graphics displays. See *virtual reality* .

artwork (1) Visual and graphic elements on a page, such as line drawings, halftones, or solids. (2) One of the outputs of a graphics system. (3) A general term applied to any artistic production.

artwork

ascender Portion of lower-case letters that extends above the main portion of the letter, such as the tops of b, d, and h.

ASCII Acronym for American Standard Code for Information Interchange. Pronounced "asskey." A 7-bit standard code adopted to facilitate interchange of data among various types of data processing and data communications equipment. Compare *EBCDIC*.

ascending order To arrange information from lowest to highest.

AS/400 Abbreviation for Application System/400, an IBM minicomputer series introduced in 1988 that replaces the System/36 and System/38.

aspect ratio In computer graphics, the relationship of the height and width of the video display screen frame or image area.

assembler Computer program that takes nonmachine-language instructions prepared by a computer user and converts them into a form that may be used by the computer. Computer program that assembles.

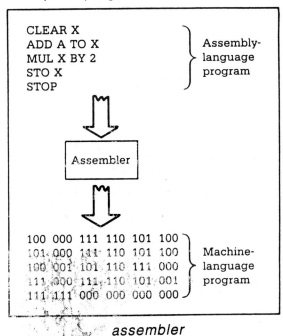

assembler

assembly language Programming language that allows a computer user to write a program using mnemonics instead of numeric instructions. A low-level symbolic programming language that closely resembles machine-code language.

Association for Computing Machinery (ACM) World's largest educational and scientific society committed to the development of technical skills and professional competence of computer specialists. Founded in 1947, ACM has earned a reputation for technical excellence by publishing prestigious journals and sponsoring numerous conferences that promote an ongoing dialogue among students, educators, and practitioners. The association is dedicated to the development of information processing as a discipline, and to the responsible use of computers in an increasing diversity of applications.

Atanasoff -Berry Computer (ABC)

Atanasoff-Berry Computer (ABC) The world's first electronic digital computer, built 1939-1942 by John V. Atanasoff and his assistant, Clifford Berry. It embodied the input, memory and arithmetic unit of future computers. See *Atanasoff, John* and *Berry, Clifford*.

Atanasoff, John Vincent (born 1903) Iowa State professor Atanasoff, with graduate student Clifford Berry, completed in 1942 the first electronic digital computer. The computer was named the ABC (Atanasoff-Berry Computer). In 1942, Atanasoff left Iowa State and the developmental work on the ABC to join the Naval Ordnance Laboratory in Washington, D.C. In 1990, nearly fifty years after his invention, Atanasoff was awarded the National Medal of Technology. See *Berry, Clifford*.

John Atanasoff

Atari Corporation Manufacturer of a popular line of personal computer systems. Atari produced several older home computers, and in 1985 introduced the Atari ST family of microcomputers. The ST computers are high-performance personal computers with capabilities for computer graphics in color.

attribute (1) The property of a graphic image that determines characteristics such as line type, line width, and color. (2) A nongraphic characteristic of a part, component, or entity under design on a CAD system. (3) A character emphasis, such as boldface and italic, or the size and font of the type.

audit trail Means for identifying the actions taken in processing input data or in preparing output. By use of the audit trail, data on a source document can be traced to a specific output and an output can be traced to the source items from which it was derived. For example, it could reveal that Nancy Wilson changed the inventory figures in the Auto Supply account at 2:32 p.m. on October 8.

authoring language A programming language that enables a non-programmer to create courseware.

authorized dealer One who is authorized by the manufacturer/developer to sell, service and support its product.

automatic backup A software program feature that automatically saves the file you are currently working on under a special name every few minutes.

automatic hyphenation A feature that hyphenates words automatically. Often found in word processing and page layout programs.

automatic pagination A feature that automatically breaks text into pages. Often found in word processing and page layout programs.

automatic reformatting In word processing, automatic adjustment of text to accommodate changes.

Automatic Sequence Controlled Calculator (ASCC) Completed in 1944 by Howard Aiken of Harvard University and the IBM Corporation, the ASCC, also called the Mark I, was an early large-scale electromechanical computer. See *Aiken, Howard.*

Automatic Sequence Controlled Calculator (ASCC)

automation (1) Implementation of processes by automatic means. (2) Automatically controlled operation of an apparatus, process, or system by mechanical or electronic devices that take the place of human observation, effort and decision.

autotrace A feature of many drawing programs that draws lines along the edges of a bit mapped image in order to convert the image into an object-oriented one. Using the autotrace tool you can transform low-resolution graphics (72 dots per inch bit-mapped image) into art that can print at substantially higher resolution (object-oriented graphics can print at the printer's maximum resolution).

A/UX A version of the UNIX operating system for the Macintosh computer. It was developed by Apple Computer, Inc.

auxiliary equipment Equipment not under direct control of the central processing unit.

auxiliary storage Storage that supplements the main storage of a computer such as hard disks, floppy disks, magnetic tapes, and optical disks.

auxiliary storage

AWK A programming language for scanning text files and processing lines or strings that match particular patterns.

B: A designation for the second floppy disk drive in IBM-compatible microcomputers. See *A:* and *C:*.

Babbage, Charles (1792-1871) British mathematician and inventor. Designed a Difference Engine for calculating logarithms to 20 decimal places and an Analytical Engine that was a forerunner of the digital computer. Babbage was ahead of his time, and the engineering techniques of his day were not advanced enough to build his machines successfully. A description of Babbage's machines would not be complete without some mention of Ada Augusta Byron. She was deeply familiar with Babbage's work and helped to document some of Babbage's efforts. See *Analytical Engine, Byran, Ada Augusta,* and *Difference Engine.*

Charles Babbage

background activity A process that does not require operator intervention but can be run by the computer while the system is used to do other work.

background color In computer graphics, a default color to which every pixel on the display is to be initialized.

backspace Keyboard operation that moves the cursor one place to the left. Allows modification of what has already been typed before it is entered into the computer.

background operations The operations occurring in the background (such as printing a document or performing a series of calculations) while you are working with an application program in the foreground.

backup (1) Pertaining to procedures or standby equipment available for use in the event of failure or overloading of the normally used procedures or equipment. (2) To make a copy of a program or data in case the original is lost, damaged, or otherwise inaccessible.

backup disk A duplicate copy of a floppy disk that preserves files in case of some disaster.

Backus, John (born 1924) In 1957, at the IBM Corporation, developed the computer language FORTRAN (FORmula TRANslator), a high-level programming language used to perform mathematical, scientific, and engineering computations. It was the first machine independent language, and it gave the computing world a quicker, cheaper, and more reliable method of programming. Backus was awarded the National Medal of Science in 1975 for his work on FORTRAN. See *FORTRAN*.

John Backus

backward compatible Compatible with earlier versions of a product.

bacteria Bacteria, also known as rabbits, are programs that do not explicitly damage any files. Their sole purpose is to reproduce themselves. A typical bacteria program does nothing more than reproduce itself exponentially, eventually eating up all the computer capacity, memory, or disk space, denying the user access to those resources. See *virus*.

bad break In desktop publishing and word processing, a place where a word, line, or page is improperly divided.

bad disk A disk that is unusable.

bad sectors During formatting of disks, all sectors are checked for usability. Unusable sectors are "flagged" as bad and are not used by the operating system. The remaining areas can then still be used.

bar chart Widely used chart in business graphics. Used to display a time schedule. Bar charts compare adjacent pieces of data and can depict individual data items side by side, stacked on top of one another, clustered together, or positioned horizontally.

bar code

bar code Code made up of a series of variable-width vertical lines which can be read by an optical bar reader. Bar codes are used to identify retail sales items, books, etc.

Bardeen, John (1908-1991)   Joined the Bell Laboratories in 1945, and shared with William Shockley and Walter Brattain the glory of the discovery of the transistor and the 1956 Nobel Prize in physics. Since 1951 he has been professor of physics at the University of Illinois and has been working on superconductivity. In 1972 he shared the Nobel Prize for a second time for his research into superconductivity. He also won such honors as the Presidential Medal of Freedom and the Soviet Academy of Sciences Lomonosovcq Prize for his work, which revolutionized technology.

John Bardeen

bar graph A graph made up of filled-in columns or rows that represent the change of data over time. Same as *bar chart*.

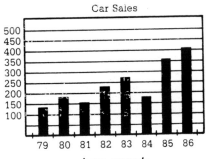

bar graph

baseband A communications system in which only one piece of information may be transferred over a link at a time.

baseline An imaginary horizontal line with which the base of each character, excluding descenders, is aligned.

BASIC Acronym for Beginner's All-purpose Symbolic Instruction Code, an easy-to-learn, easy-to-use, algebraic programming language with a small repertory of commands and simple statement formats. Developed at Dartmouth College by John Kemeny and Thomas Kurtz. Widely used in programming instruction, in personal computing, and in business and industry. The language has changed over the years. Early versions are unstructured and interpreted. Later versions are structured and often compiled.

```
REM  Fibonacci numbers

LIBRARY "numlib.trc"
DIM F(16)

CALL Fibonacci(F)
MAT PRINT F;

FOR n = 2 to 15
    PRINT F(n)*F(n) - F(n-1)*F(n+1);
NEXT n

END
```
BASIC program

basic input-output system (BIOS) A set of programs encoded in read-only memory (ROM) in IBM-compatible microcomputers. These programs facilitate the transfer of data and control instructions between the computer and peripherals.

batch file A file that contains a series of commands to be processed sequentially.

batch mode A job entry mode in which the entire job is entered at one time from a disk drive, tape drive, or card reader.

batch processing (1) Technique by which programs to be executed are coded and collected together for processing in groups or patches. The user gives the job to a computer center, where it is put into a batch of programs and processed, and then returned. The user has no direct access to the machine. See *remote batch processing*. (2) Processing as a group data that has been accumulated over a period of time or must be done periodically, as in payroll and billing applications.

baud A unit for measuring data transmission speed. It is the number of bits (binary digits) the computer will send per second. The higher the baud rate, the greater the amount of information exchanged per second.

baud rate The speed at which telecommunicated data is transmitted, measured in bits per second. Common baud rates are 9,600 and 14,400.

BBS Acronym for Bulletin Board System. Enables users to log into another computer system from remote terminals. Many of these BBSs can be used free of charge and can be reached by modem.

Bell Laboratories The research and development center of the AT & T Company and one of the most renowned scientific laboratories in the world. Many computer hardware developments and software concepts and programs were generated at Bell Laboratories.

benchmark Point of reference from which measurements can be made, such as use of a program to evaluate the performance of a computer. Any standard against which products can be compared.

Bernoulli box A removable hard disk system for microcomputers, manufactured by Iomega Corporation. The main advantage of this cartridge system is that one hard disk system can be used for multiple libraries of hard disk data.

Berry, Clifford (died 1963) In 1942, with Iowa State professor John Atanasoff, completed the first electronic digital computer. The computer was named the ABC (Atanasoff-Berry Computer) and it embodied the input, memory and arithmetic unit of future computers. Berry earned a Ph.D. in physics at Iowa State and eventually became director of engineering for the analytical and control instrument division of Consolidated Electrodynamics. See *Atanasoff-Berry Computer* and *Atanasoff, John.*

Clifford Berry

berserk Refers to the fit of rage computer users go into when their computer fails to work the way they thought it would.

beta test The product test stage following alpha test during which a new product is tested under actual usage conditions in a customer environment. Software testing by first-time users. See *alpha test.*

31

GREENSBORO DAY SCHOOL

Bezier curve A type of curve generated by an algorithm. Named after French mathematician Pierre Bezier, it is used to display nonuniform curves based upon a fitting algorithm. Bezier curves need only a few points to define a large number of shapes, hence their usefulness over other mathematical methods for approximating a given shape. Within drawing programs, Bezier curves are typically reshaped by moving the handles that appear off of the curve. Originated around 1962 for use in car body design in France.

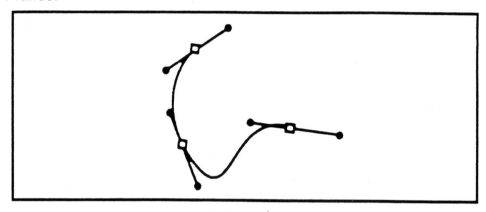

Bezier curve

bidirectional bus Refers to a data bus that can transmit data in either direction. The bus also carries special signals that inform the devices connected to it which way data are passing.

bidirectional printer Printer that prints from left to right as well as from right to left, avoiding carriage-return delay.

binary

binary Mathematical representation of a number to the base 2, i.e., with only two states, 1 and 0; ON and OFF; or HIGH or LOW. Requires a greater number of digits than base 10, i.e. 254 = 11111110.

binary logic A system of logic built around comparisons between two bits.

BIOS See *basic input-output system*.

bit The smallest unit of information that can be stored and processed by a computer.

bit flipping Process of inverting bits — changing 1s to 0s and vice versa. For example, in a graphics program, to invert a black-and-white bit-mapped image (to change black to white and vice versa), the program could simply flip the bits that makeup the bit map.

bit image Collection of bits stored in a computer's memory, arranged into a rectangular matrix. The computer's display screen is a bit image that is visible to the user.

bit map A data structure that describes a bit image being held in computer storage. Each picture element (pixel) is represented by bits stored in the memory. Bit-mapped graphics are notorious for using lots of memory. Up to a million bytes of memory may be required to store a bit map or a high-resolution black/white screen display; several million bytes may be required to store a bit map for a full page color image.

bit mapped font A set of characters in a particular size and style, in which each character is described in a unique bit map (pattern of dots). Bit mapped screen or printer fonts represent characters with a matrix of dots. To display or print bit-mapped fonts, the computer or printer must keep a full representation of each character in memory.

bit mapped graphics

bit mapped graphics A method of generating screen images by creating a one-for-one correspondence between bits in memory and pixels on the screen. In color graphics, three or more bits are required in the bit map to represent the red, green, and blue values of an individual pixel. Bit mapped graphics are created by paint programs and some scanners.

BITNET An acronym for Because It's Time NETwork, a wide area network that connects more than a thousand colleges and universities in the United States, Canada, and Europe.

BITS An acronym for Boot Integrity Token System, a smartcard protected operating system. The basic idea behind BITS is that the host computer will actually boot from a smartcard.

bits per second (bps) Refers to the number of bits of information transferred per second. See *baud rate*.

BIX An acronym for Byte Information Exchange, an on-line commercial information service that was spawned by BYTE magazine.

blend A feature on many digital painting programs that lets you soften the edges or mix colors where two objects or regions meet.

blinking (1) Graphics aid that makes a predefined graphic entity blink on the CRT to attract the designer's attention. (2) A means of highlighting a graphics object or text by changing the color or intensity between two values periodically.

block A string of data elements recorded or transmitted as a unit.

block operation Operations that can be performed on a selected area of text, such moving a block of data or changing the type style of a block of data.

blow-up (1) The changing of a smaller format picture into a larger format picture. (2) Unexpected halt to a program due to a bug or because it encounters data conditions it cannot handle.

boilerplate Pieces of text that get used over and over again, word for word, in different documents.

boldface A type font in which the main strokes of the letter are thicker than normal. Printed characters in darker type than the surrounding characters.

bomb (1) A concealed fault that can cause a system to crash. (2) To sabotage a system by deliberately writing a program that will disrupt the system. (3) To fail suddenly and completely. See *crash*.

Boolean algebra Branch of symbolic logic similar in form to algebra, but dealing with logical relationships instead of numerical relationships.It lay dormant until it could be usefully applied to the fields of relay switching and electronic computers, but has now become an important subject in the logic design of electronic computers. Named for George Boole.

Boole, George (1815-1864)   British logician and mathematician. In 1847, wrote a pamphlet called "Mathematical Analysis of Logic." In 1851, wrote a more mature statement of his logical system in a larger work, "An Investigation of the Laws of Thought," in which are founded the mathematical theories of logic. Boole's discovery that the symbolism of algebra could be used in logic has had wide impact in the twentieth century. Today, Boolean algebra is important not only in logic but also in the theory of probability, the geometry of sets and information theory. It has also led to the design of electronic computers through the interpretation of Boolean combinations of sets as switching circuits. See *Boolean algebra*.

George Boole

boot   To start up a computer. Microcomputers have a bootstrap routine in a ROM chip that is automatically executed when the computer is turned on or reset. It searches for the operating system, loads it and than passes control over to it.

bootstrapping   Starting a computer system. "Cold boot" means complete restarting after switching the power on, while "warm boot" means partial restarting under operating system control.

Borland International Inc.   A leading microcomputer software company. Founded in 1983 by Philippe Kahn, Borland introduced Turbo Pascal, which instantly became a popular commercial product. Borland has continued to develop popular software products.

bps   See *bits per second*.

branch   Selection of one or more possible paths in the flow of control, based on some criterion. Programming instruction that causes transfer of control to another program sequence.

break (1) Interruption of a transmission. (2) To interrupt execution of a program.

Brattain, Walter Houser (1902-1987) Joined the Bell Laboratories in 1929, and shared with John Bardeen and William Shockley the discovery of the transistor and the 1956 Nobel Prize in Physics. Brattain has also done research on piezoelectric frequency standards, magnetometers, infrared detectors, and blood clotting. He worked as a research physicist until his retirement in 1967. Brattain was a visiting professor at Whitman College (where he obtained his BS degree) from 1962-72.

Walter Brattain

Bricklin, Daniel (born 1951) Developed the first electronic spreadsheet, VisiCalc, in 1978. VisiCalc is a software package that helps businesses in their financial planning by showing the overall results of various shifts in capital. The spreadsheet concept was so popular in the early 1980s that it actually helped sell personal computers. By early 1983 approximately 400,000 copies of VisiCalc were in consumer hands. Today, electronic spreadsheets are one of the most popular programs used with personal computers. See *VisiCalc*.

Daniel Bricklin

bridge A device connecting two networks, which may or may not be using the same hardware protocol (i.e. Ethernet or ARCnet), but must be using the same network operating system.

broadband A communications system in which multiple messages may be simultaneously transferred over a path.

broadcast To send information, particularly data packets, on a network.

brownout An extended period of insufficient power line voltage. It can damage computer equipment.

browse To view information without manipulating it.

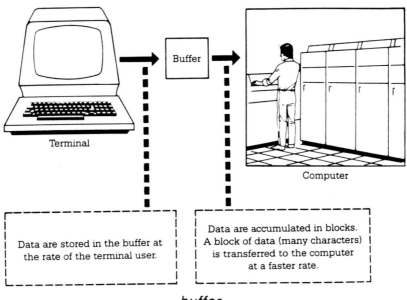

Terminal

Computer

Data are stored in the buffer at the rate of the terminal user.

Data are accumulated in blocks. A block of data (many characters) is transferred to the computer at a faster rate.

buffer

buffer A holding area for data.

bug A flaw in the design or implementation of a software program or hardware design which causes erroneous results or malfunctions.

built-in font A printer font encoded permanently in the printer's read-only memory (ROM).

built-in function In a spreadsheet, a predetermined formula that performs a time-consuming calculation.

bulletin board system (BBS) A service that permits individuals who have personal computers to communicate with others who have similar interests. Individuals who subscribe to the service can retrieve information from a common database.

bundled software Software included with a computer system as part of the systems' total price. Contrast with *unbundled software*.

bunny suit Protective clothing worn by individuals in a clean room that keeps human bacteria from infecting the chip-making process.

burn-in Process of testing computers, microprocessors, memory chips and other components by running the equipment for an extended period. This testing process causes weak links in the equipment to burn out, the failed equipment is replaced with components that will withstand the test.

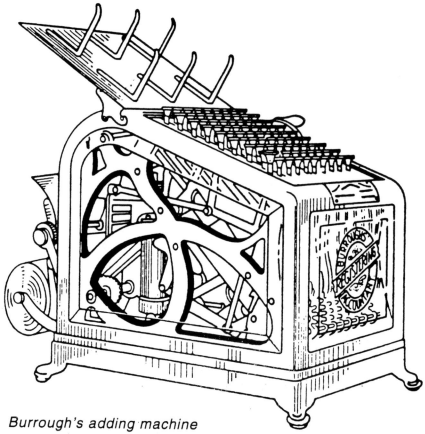

Burrough's adding machine

Burroughs, William Seward (1857-1898)
Inventor of adding and calculating machines,
patented in 1892 the first commercial
successful adding machine. With Dorr E. Felt,
Burroughs pioneered the development of
adding machines by the provision for the first
time of a full keyboard. Burroughs' unique
contribution was the addition of a printing
device to record numbers and totals. The
company he founded grew into one of the
world's major computer manufacturers,
Burroughs Corporation (now Unisys
Corporation).

William Burroughs

bus The main communication avenue in a computer. An internal pathway
along which signals are sent from one part of the computer to another.

bus architecture The overall structure of a data bus system in a particular
type of computer system.

Bush, Vannevar (1890-1974) Trying to solve differential equations associated with power failures, he built, in 1930, the first automatic computer general enough to solve a wide variety of problems. Called a "differential analyzer," this forerunner of present-day analog computers weighed 100 tons and used thousands of vacuum tubes. Analog machines like this, but rather simpler, were widely used in World War II for radar and gun operations.

Vannevar Bush

Bushnell, Nolan In 1972, started Atari Corporation and introduced computerized game playing. Although his first game, Computer Space, was a commercial flop, he then developed many successful games: Pong, Pac Man, Space Invaders, Asteroids and Missile Command. The video games were so successful that Warner Communications bought Atari for $28 million in 1976. Bushnell went on to develop many other products and establish several new companies.

Nolan Bushnell

business graphics (1) Pie charts, bar charts, scattergrams, graphs, and other visual representations of the operational or strategic aspects of a business such as sales vs. costs, sales by department, comparative product performance, and stock prices. (2) Applications programs that allow the user to display data as visual presentations. (3) With the advent of low-cost computers, graphics packages are now available for creating business graphics where virtually any type of data set can be displayed as graphs, charts, and histograms.

business graphics

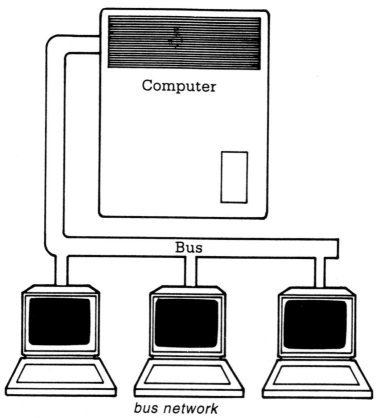

bus network

bus network One of the three principal topologies for a local area network, in which all stations, or computer devices, communicate by using a common distribution channel, or bus. See *network, ring network* and *star network*.

Byron, Ada Augusta (1815-1852) Ada Byron, Countess of Lovelace, developed the essential ideas of programming. A skilled mathematician and close friend of Charles Babbage, she wrote about his machine: "The Analytical Engine weaves algebraic patterns just as the Jacquard loom weaves flowers and leaves." The U.S. Pentagon has honored Ada Augusta Byron by naming a high-level programming language Ada. Ada is a Pascal-based language that is very comprehensive. See *Ada* and *Babbage, Charles*.

Ada Byron

byte Eight binary bits of data grouped together to represent a character, digit or other value. A common unit of computer storage from personal computers to mainframe computers.

C Full name of a programming language designed for use on microcomputers. Combines high-level statements with low-level machine control to deliver software that is both easy to use and highly efficient. It is very popular with system programmers because of its transportability between computer systems. C was developed by Dennis Ritchie and Brian Kernighan at Bell Laboratories in the early 1970s. The language is closely associated with the Unix operating system, now widely used by professional programmers. The language is capable of providing especially concise and efficient code.

```
double inner (v1,v2,n)
double v1 ( ), v2 ( );
        double sum;
        int i;
        sum = 0.0;
        for (i=0; i<n; i ++)
            sum = + V1(i), v2(i);
        return (sum);
```

C program

C++ An object-oriented version of the C programming language, developed by Bjarne Stroustrup in the early 1980s at Bell Laboratories. The language has been chosen by several large software publishers for major development projects. The term C++ means "more than C."

© Copyright symbol indicating the exclusive right granted by law to sell, distribute, or reproduce a graphic image or document.

C: A designation for the primary hard disk in IBM-compatible microcomputers. See *A:* and *B:*.

cabling The physical medium that connects the elements of a network, enabling them to communicate.

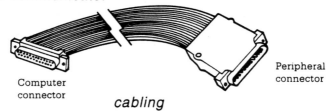

Computer connector

Peripheral connector

cabling

cache A faster memory in which parts of the information in the main (slower) memory or disk are copied. Information that is likely to require reading or alteration goes to the cache, where the system can access it more quickly. Caching can significantly speed processing of some programs, especially if floppy disks are used for mass storage.

CAD See *computer-aided design*.

CAD/CAM An acronym for Computer Aided Design/Computer Assisted Manufacturing, a group of programs that are used by designers and engineers to help draw products (such as automobiles, circuit boards, windsurfers or farm tools) that are to be built. CAM refers to programs that tell machines what to do in the manufacturing process.

CAI See *computer assisted instruction*.

calculator Any mechanical or electronic machine used for performing calculations. Calculators, as distinguished from computers, usually require frequent human intervention.

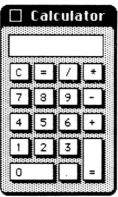

calculator

CAM Acronym for Computer Aided Manufacturing. The use of computers to assist in any or all phases of manufacturing.

cancel (1) Keyboard operation that deletes the line currently being typed. (2) To end a task before it is completed.

canned software Programs prepared by computer manufacturers or software developers and provided to a user in ready-to-use form. General enough to be used by many businesses and individuals. Contrast with *custom software*.

capacity Number of items of data that a storage device is capable of containing. Frequently defined in terms of computer words, bytes, or characters.

caps Capital letters. All caps means that all letters are capitalized; initial caps means the capitalization of the first letter of each significant word. ALL CAPS WOULD LOOK LIKE THIS.

card (1)Printed circuit board. (2) Storage medium in which data are represented by means of holes punched in vertical columns in a 7.37 inch by 3.25 inch (18.7 cm by 8.3 cm) paper card.

carpel-tunnel syndrome A type of repetitive stress injury that affects the wrist. Repeated and prolonged typing at a keyboard can cause this serious disorder.

carriage return (CR) In a printer the operation that causes the next character to be printed at the left margin.

cartridge A generic term that can refer to any of several devices that are self-contained, usually in some kind of plastic housing. For example, ROM cartridge, disk cartridge, toner cartridge, memory cartridge, tape cartridge, or font cartridge.

cascading windows Overlapping on-screen windows.

catalog A list of the contents of a disk or magnetic tape.

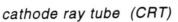

cathode ray tube (CRT)

cathode ray tube (CRT) Electronic tube with a screen upon which information may be displayed.

CBT See *computer-based training*.

CD-ROM An acronym for Compact Disc Read-Only Memory, a type of optical disk that uses the same basic technology as do the popular CD audio disks. Although a CD-ROM drive can only read data (the data is permanently stamped onto the disks during manufacturing), the disks are inexpensive to make and can each hold about 650 megabytes of data. Contents are typically an entire encyclopedia on a single CD, a set of reference works, a clip-art library, a collection of fine art, or any other publication which is for reading only.

CD-ROM

cel animation An animation technique in which a background painting is held stationary while animated images are moved over the painting, producing the illusion of movement. Animation programs are available that perform cel animation.

cell (1) Storage for one unit of information, usually one character, one byte, or one word. A binary cell is a cell of one binary digit capacity. (2) Single coordinate location within the grid, or matrix, that constitutes the basic form of an electronic spreadsheet.

cell address In a spreadsheet, the column and row coordinates of a cell.

central processing unit (CPU) A processor that contains the sequencing and processing facilities for instruction execution, timing functions, initial program loading, and other machine-related functions. The computing part of the computer.

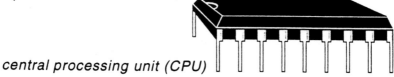

central processing unit (CPU)

44

Centronics interface A de facto standard for parallel data exchange paths between computers and peripherals. Centronics Corporation was one of the original printer manufacturers to use the parallel scheme for communications between computers and printers. The 36-pin parallel interface was introduced in 1970.

CG An acronym for Computer Graphics, any graphical element created with the aid of a computer.

CGA Acronym for Color Graphics Adapter. The original low-resolution color standard for IBM compatible microcomputers, introduced by the IBM Corporation in 1981. The CGA is capable of several character and graphics modes. CGA has been superseded by EGA and VGA.

character Any symbol, digit, letter, or punctuation mark — including the blank character — stored or processed by computing equipment.

character attribute A character emphasis, such as **boldface** and *italic*, or the size and font of the type.

character recognition Technology of using machines to identify human-readable symbols automatically, and then to express their identities in machine-readable codes. This operation of transforming numbers and letters into a form directly suitable for data processing is an important method of introducing information into computing systems.

characters per inch Method of expressing the output from printers as determined by type size and style. Abbreviated cpi.

characters per second Unit for measuring output of low-speed serial printers. Abbreviated cps.

chart Visual representation of quantitative information — such as a bar graph, in which the information is made visual by heavy horizontal or vertical lines, or a circle graph or pie chart, in which the information is pictured as slices of an imaginary pie.

checksum Summation of digits or bits used primarily for checking purposes and summed according to an arbitrary set of rules. Used to verify the integrity of data.

children In hierarchical databases, those data elements that are linked in a subordinate fashion to a parent element.

chip A miniaturized electronic circuit. They hold from a few dozen to several million electronic components (transistors, resistors, etc.). See *DIP, PGA, SIMM* and *SIP*.

circuit board Thin insulating board used to mount and connect various electronic components and microchips in a pattern of conductive lines. This circuit pattern is etched into the board's surface.

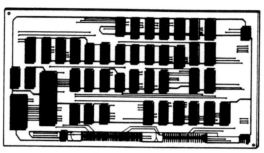

circuit board

clear (1) Keyboard function that removes the contents from the display screen. (2) Same as zap.

click To point the mouse pointer at a word or icon on the screen, press the mouse button, and then release it quickly. Clicking is usually performed to select or deselect an item or to activate a program or program feature.

client Any computer using the services of a computer network.

client/server system A computer system in which personal computers or workstations function as "clients" that request services from print servers, file servers, database servers, etc., which may be located at remote sites.

clip To select a part of a graphic to show on the screen or place into a document. Clipping is used to select a region of interest rather than scaling the entire image.

clip art Collections of pictures and design elements (such as borders, symbols, drawings, etc). The collections may be in printed form or stored on diskettes or CD-ROM. This pre-drawn artwork can be used in designing newsletters, brochures, flyers, books, magazines and incorporated into other documents.

clipboard A temporary holding place that facilitates the cutting and pasting of text and graphics. Clipboard information is held in memory only while the computer is turned on. A clipboard allows information to be transferred from

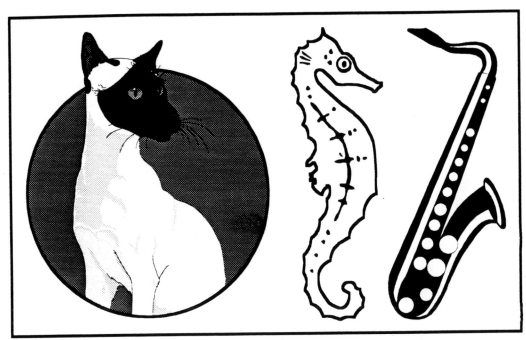

clip art

one program to another. A clipboard stores a copy of the last information that was "copied" or "cut." A "paste" operation passes data from the clipboard to the current program.

clock speed The internal heartbeat of a computer, governing the speed of the processor. For example, the same processor running at 40 megahertz (million cycles per second) is twice as fast internally as one running at 20 megahertz.

clone Technically, a clone is an identical copy of some device. With regard to computers, a clone is a compatible computer that is capable of running the same software as the original machine. It also implies the machine can use similar components as the original, although this is not always true. Several clone computers exist for IBM Personal Computers. In 1995, Power Computing Corporation announced a clone for the Apple Macintosh. Power Computing was founded in 1994 by Korean-American engineer Stephen Kahng, who a decade ago designed the Leading Edge computer that helped launch the PC clone industry.

close To finish and save.

closed architecture Personal computer design that limits add-ons to those that can be plugged into the back of the machine. See *open system*.

cluster A station that consists of a control unit and the terminals connected to it.

CMOS An abbreviation for Complementary Metal-Oxide Semiconductor, a technology for making integrated circuits that use very little power. This technology is popular both for portables and for desktop computers, partly because it produces less heat than other integrated circuits. Invented by Frank Wanlass in the mid-1960s.

coaxial cable Two electrical conductors sharing the same core, one wire arranged to shield or surround the other. Used for communications connections between different pieces of equipment.

COBOL Acronym for COmmon Business-Oriented Language, a high-level language developed for business data processing applications. Every COBOL source program has four divisions: (1) Identification Division identifies the source program and output of a compilation; (2) Environment Division specifies those aspects of a data processing problem that are dependent upon the physical characteristics of a particular computer; (3) Data Division describes the data that the object program is to accept as input, manipulate, create, or produce as output; and (4) Procedure Division specifies the procedures to be performed by the object program, using English-like statements.

```
100    PROCEDURE DIVISION
110    PGM-VWGIN.MOVE ZEROS TO TOTAL-COUNT, INC.
120    LOOP. IF INC IS GREATER THAN 100
130        GO TO PGM-END.
140      ADD 1 TO INC.
150      ADD INC TO TOTAL-COUNT.
160      GO TO LOOP.
170    PGM-END. STOP RUN.
```

COBOL program

coding (1) Writing a list of instructions that will cause a computer to perform specified operations. (2) Ordered list or lists of the successive instructions that will cause a computer to perform a particular process.

cold boot A computer start-up that begins when the power is turned on.

collate To put things in a certain order.

color graphics Any type of computer graphic in which the images displayed on a visual display screen, printed copy, or other type of display are shown in more than one color.

color graphics adapter (CGA) An adapter that simultaneously provides four colors. It allows a computer to show color graphics as well as text.

color monitor A computer display designed to work with a video card or adapter to produce text or graphics image in color. A color monitor has a screen coated internally with three phosphors — one each for red, green and blue. To light the phosphor and produce a spot of color, such a monitor also usually contains three electron guns — again, one for each of the three colors.

color resolution The number of different colors or gray-scale values a system can produce or work with. A value is usually given in bits.

color separation The creation of a multicolor graphic by creating several layers, with each layer corresponding to one of the colors that will be printed when the graphic is reproduced by a commercial printer.

column (1) Vertical numbers of one line of an array. (2) One of the vertical lines of punching positions on a punched card. (3) Position of information in a computer word. (4) Horizontal division of an electronic spreadsheet. Together with rows, columns serve to form the spreadsheet matrix. Contrast with *row*.

COMDEX An acronym for COMputer Dealer's EXposition, the largest computer trade show in the world. Held in the United States and in other locations throughout the world.

command (1) Control signal. (2) Loosely, a mathematical or logic operator. (3) Loosely, a computer instruction.

command language Language used to give instructions to an operating system.

Commodore Business Machines, Inc. Manufacturer of the Amiga family of microcomputers and several older microcomputers including the popular Commodore 64. Discontinued manufacturing computers in 1994.

communication satellite An earth orbiting device capable fo relaying communication signals over long distances. Computer systems use satellites to communicate from one country to another.

communications program A computer program that allows a computer to communicate with other computers through modems and the telephone network.

communications protocol Set of communication rules that provides for error checking between devices and ensures that transmitted data are not lost.

Compaq Computer Corporation A manufacturer of IBM-compatible microcomputers. Founded in 1982, Compaq has become an industry leader and is known for producing reliable computers.

compatible Refers to two machines capable of using the same software as well as the same hardware components.

compiler A program that converts, or translates, symbolic commands into instructions that can be executed by a computer.

compress To save storage space by eliminating gaps, empty fields, redundancy or unnecessary data to shorten the length of records or files.

CompuServe Major information service network used by individuals as well as businesses. Carries timely news features, stock market reports, electronic mail, educational programs, legal advice, travel reservations, encyclopedia references, games, programming aids, and more. Personal computer owners can reference the CompuServe network via the common telephone system. See *on-line information service*.

compute bound A computer is said to be "compute bound" if the amount of work it can do is limited by the rate at which its CPU can perform calculations.

computer Device capable of solving problems or manipulating data by accepting data, performing prescribed operations (mathematical or logical) on the data, and supplying the results of these operations.

computer

computer accessories The equipment that can be attached to a computer, such as mouse, disk drive, visual display device, keyboard, or printer.

computer-aided design (CAD) Computer systems and programs used in designing tools, automobiles, buildings, aircraft, molecules, farm equipment, integrated circuits, and thousands of other products. Computer-aided design has become a mainstay in a variety of design related fields, such as architecture, mechanical engineering, interior design, civil engineering and electrical engineering. CAD applications are graphics and calculation-intensive, requiring fast computers and high-resolution video displays.

computer-aided design (CAD)

computer-animated graphics In multimedia applications, graphics animated by means of a computer, rather than film or videotape.

computer animation Animation produced with the use of a software program and a computer. Computer animation makes possible an added dimension in which there are no rules for time and space, light and color, or for obeying the laws of Physics as known to Newton or Einstein. No other medium has given artists such complete control and achieved such stunning results. Computer animation can take either two-dimensional or three-dimensional form. Two-dimensional animation uses flat images for creating characters and/or backgrounds. Three-dimensional animation requires modeling or model design. Geometric models are stored in a computer and can be rotated, translated and scaled as needed to create and manipulate images. More sophisticated three-dimensional animation system allow the design and manipulation of complex scenes and characters for film making.

computer art

computer art A broad term that can refer either to art created on a computer or to art generated by the computer, the difference being whether the artist is human or electronic. When created by human beings, computer art is done with painting and drawing programs that offer a range of drawing tools, brushes, pencils, patterns, shapes, and colors. The artist can dream lovely images and use the computer to bring them to vivid reality.

computer artist Person who uses computers as tools in producing art.

computer-based training (CBT) Training that uses interactive computer programs to teach new skills. An interactive program is like a very patient teacher.

computer center Facility that provides computer services to a variety of users through the operation of computer and auxiliary hardware, and through ancillary services provided by its staff.

computer chess A program that plays chess. Most computer chess programs combine brute force and selective search algorithms. Cray Blitz, the most brute force-like program, looks at 100 million chess positions per move, whereas BP, a personal computer based program, looks at only 2400 positions per move. Socrates II triumphed over 11 other computer chess programs at the 1993 ACM's Annual International Computer Chess Championship. Socrates II runs on an IBM-compatible computer. Computer chess is becoming an artificial intelligence testbed and is raising some important questions, such as: Why can't a computer that searches billions of positions per second compete against the best humans?

computer classifications Digital computers are broken down into three classifications: mainframes (which includes supercomputers), minicomputers and microcomputers.

computer crime The unauthorized use of computer systems including software or data, for unlawful purposes.

computerese Jargon and other specialized vocabulary of people working with computers and information processing systems.

computer family A term commonly used to indicate a group of computers that are built around the same central processing unit, same microprocessor, or around a series of related microprocessors and that share significant design features. For example, the IBM PC and IBM PS/2 models represent a family designed by IBM Corporation around the Intel 80x86 series of microprocessors (80286, 80386 and 80486).

computer graphics General term meaning the appearance of pictures or diagrams, as distinct from letters and numbers, on the display screen or hard-copy output device. The term computer graphics encompasses different methods of generating, displaying, and storing information.

computer graphics

computer graphics artist A person who uses computers as tools in producing commercial art and fine art.

computerize To automate by means of computer systems.

computer jargon Technical vocabulary associated with the computer field.

computer language A means of communication. It is used to tell a computer what to do and how to do it. Computer language is also called programming language. The most popular high-level programming language is BASIC.

```
program Craps;
var
  Die1, Die2, Roll       :Integer;
begin
  Write('Enter the dice numbers: ');
  ReadLn(Die1, Die2);
  Roll := Die1 + Die2;
  case Roll of
    2, 3, 12 : WriteLn('Craps');
    4, 10    : WriteLn('Point = ', Roll);
    5, 9     : WriteLn('Point = ', Roll);
    6, 8     : WriteLn('Point = ', Roll);
    7, 11    : WriteLn('Win')
  end (**** of case statement ****)
end.
```

computer language

computer literacy A broad knowledge of how to use computers to solve problems, general awareness of the functioning of the software and hardware, and an understanding of the societal implications of computers.

Computer Museum Archive for computer history, located in Boston, Massachusetts, whose collection contains many early computer systems and taped presentations of computer pioneers.

computer network An interconnected complex of two or more computer systems.

computer operator Person skilled in the operation of the computer and associated peripheral devices. Performs other operational functions that are required in a computer center, such as loading a disk drive, removing printouts from the line printer rack, and sometimes bursting and decollating.

computer program A specific set of software commands in a form acceptable to a computer and used to achieve a desired result.

computer programmer Person whose job is to design, write, and test programs that cause a computer to do a specific job.

computer resource Any of the computer system elements needed to perform required operations, including software, data files, processing units, input-output units, storage units and operating personnel.

computer science Field of knowledge embracing all aspects of the design and use of computers. Aspects of computer science range from programming and computer graphics to artificial intelligence and robotics. Offered as a degree program in many colleges and universities.

computer security Preservation of computing resources against abuse or unauthorized use, especially the protection of data from accidental or deliberate damage, disclosure, or modification.

computer simulation The representation of a system by a computer program. For example, a program to simulate the growth of plants, or a trip to a far away planet.

computer store Retail store where customers can select, from the shelf or the floor, a full computer system or just a few accessories. These stores typically sell software, books, supplies, and periodicals. In a broad-based computer store, one can examine and operate several types of microcomputer systems.

computer store

computer system System that includes computer hardware, software, and people. Used to process data into useful information.

computer user Any person who uses a computer system or its output.

computer users group Group whose members share the knowledge they have gained and the programs they have developed on a computer or class of computers of a certain manufacturer. Most groups hold meetings and distribute newsletters to exchange information, trade equipment, and share computer programs.

computer vendor Organization that manufactures, sells, or services computer equipment.

computer virus A program that attaches itself to other programs or data. A virus' typical purpose is to disrupt the processing of information on an infected system. When an infected program is executed, the virus reproduces and spreads by searching for other software that is not infected, and then attaching itself to previously "clean" software.

computer vision In artificial intelligence, the design of computer systems to make sense of visual images.

Computerworld A weekly publication that provides articles and advertisements regarding topics of interest, such as word processing, robotics, office automation, programming languages, computer company stock quotes, information systems, etc.

computing Act of using computing equipment for processing data. Art or science of getting the computer to do what the user wants.

computing power The relative speed of computing. One computer is described as being more powerful than another if it can handle more work at a faster speed.

concatenate To link together or join two or more character strings into a single character string, or to join one line of a display with the succeeding line. To compress.

condensed type Type narrowed in width so that more characters will fit into a linear inch.

conditional statement Statement that is executed only when a certain condition within the routine has been met.

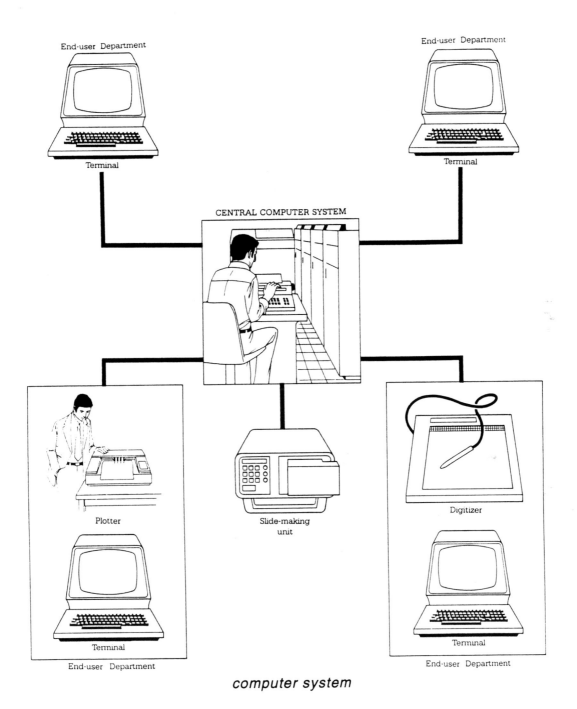

computer system

configuration (1) A particular arrangement of computer equipment, including a computer, peripherals, and interfaces, all of which will work efficiently together. (2) Layout or design of elements in a hardware or computer graphics system.

constant (1) Value that does not change during the execution of the program. (2) In a spreadsheet, a number you type directly into a cell or place in a formula.

contiguous Adjacent or adjoining.

continuous forms Fanfold paper or roll paper that has small holes on the outer edges for automatic feeding into printers. Can be blank sheets or preprinted forms such as checks, invoices, or tax forms.

Control Data Corporation One of the first computer companies. It was founded by William C. Norris in 1957. Control Data has always specialized in manufacturing large mainframe computers and supercomputers. See *Norris, William.*

control key Special-function key on a computer keyboard. Used simultaneously with another key to enter a command instructing the system to perform a task.

controller Within the computer, the controller is a hardware device that controls the activities of peripheral devices such as a disk drive or display terminal.

control panel That part of a computer control console that contains manual controls.

conversion (1) Process of changing information from one form of representation to another, such as from the language of one type of computer to that of another or from a scanned image to magnetic disk. (2) Process of changing from one data processing method to another or from one type of equipment to another. (3) Process of changing a number written in one base to the base of another numeral system.

coprocessor A device that performs specialized processing in conjunction with the main microprocessor of a system. It works in tandem with another central processing unit to increase the computing power of a system. An extra microprocessor to handle some things faster than the main processor, i.e., a math coprocessor or a graphics coprocessor.

copy To reproduce data in a new location or other destination, leaving the source data unchanged, although the physical form of the result may differ from that of the source; for example, to make a duplicate of all the programs or data on a disk, or to copy a graphic screen image to a printer.

copy protection Methods used by software developers to prevent any copying of their programs. To protect against illegal copying of software, many software developers build copy-protection routines into their programs. Copy-protection techniques are sometimes sophisticated, although several commercial programs exist that allow users to override many standard copy-protection techniques.

copyright Recognized ownership of creative work; protection against unauthorized use of work.

copyright notice A notification of copyright that is part of a program and is often printed on the display screen at the start of the program. It reminds the user that the program has a copyright, and that making copies for any purpose other than for backup is illegal.

Corbató, Fernando J. (born 1926) Organized the concepts and led the development of the general-purpose large-scale time-sharing and resource-sharing computer systems CTSS and Multics. He was the recipient of the ACM 1990 A.M. Turing Award, the Association of Computing Machinery's highest honor for technical achievements in computer science and information technology. Corbato was born in 1926 and was associated with the MIT Computation Center from 1956-1966. In 1982 he was the charter recipient of the IEEE Computer Pioneer Award.

Fernando Corbato

Corel Draw An illustrative graphics program which runs on Windows. It was introduced in 1989 by Corel Systems Corporation. Corel Draw includes hundreds of precision fonts, many clip art and photo CD-ROMs, and is known for its speed and ease of use.

corrupted file A file with distorted data.

courseware The name of computer programs that are used to teach educational subjects in schools.

cpi See *characters per inch.*

cps See *characters per second.*

cpu See *central processing unit.*

crash

crash (1) An unplanned program termination due to a hardware or software failure. (2) A failure of a program or a disk drive, usually causing the loss of data. See *bomb*.

Cray Research, Inc. A manufacturer of supercomputers founded in 1972 by Seymour Cray, a leading designer of mainframes at Control Data Corporation. In 1976, Cray Research sold its first supercomputer, the Cray 1, to Los Alamos National Laboratories. Cray supercomputers are multi-million dollar machines that are typically used for the most complex computational tasks. See *Cray, Seymour*.

Cray, Seymour (born 1925) Founded Cray Research, Inc. in 1972 for the purpose of developing supercomputers. Introduced the world's first commercial supercomputer, the Cray 1, in 1976. It could perform 160 million calculations per second. He designed the Cray 2, twelve times faster than the Cray 1, and released it in 1985. In 1989, Seymour Cray left Cray Research and founded Cray Computer Corporation. Cray has invented a number of technologies that have been patented by the companies for which he has worked. Among the more significant are the Cray 1 vector register technology, the cooling technologies for the Cray 2, and the CDC 6600 Freon-cooling system. The 8-billion byte Cray 3 supercomputer is his latest creation. For over 30 years his name has been synonymous with the stratosphere in high performance computing. See *Cray Research, Inc.*

Seymour Cray

crop To trim a graphics image for a better fit or to eliminate unwanted portions. In preparing an illustration for traditional printing, cropping is used to clean up a graphic for placement in a document.

crosshair cursor A digitizing device that is often moved over hard-copy images of maps and drawings to enter those images into the computer system.

cross assembler An assembler that runs on one computer, producing code for a different computer.

crosshatching In computer graphics, the shading of some portion of a drawing with a pattern of intersecting lines or figures repeated across the area being shaded. Crosshatching is one of several methods for filling in areas of a graphic.

CRT

CRT Acronym for Cathode Ray Tube, the picture tube of the standard computer display screen. A CRT display is built around a vacuum tube containing one or more electron guns whose electron beams rapidly sweep horizontally across the inside of the front surface of the tube, which is coated with a material that glows when irradiated.

current cell The cell currently available for use on a spreadsheet.

current directory The directory that an operating system or application program uses by default to store and retrieve files.

current drive The disk drive currently being used by the computer system.

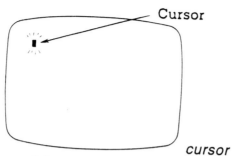

Cursor

cursor

cursor (1) Moving, sliding, or blinking symbol on a CRT screen that indicates where the next character will appear. (2) Position indicator used on a video display terminal to indicate a character to be connected or a position in which data is to be entered. (3) On graphic systems, it can take any shape (arrow, square, paintbrush, etc.) and is used to mark where the next graphic action is to take place.

custom software Software designed and programmed for a customer, in contrast with software that is available off the shelf for a particular use such as accounting or graphics.

cut Act of removing text or graphics from a document.

cut and paste Method employed by some systems to move graphics and/ or text from one location to another. Such systems usually permit the performance of other operations between the cut and the paste steps. Cut and paste enables compatible programs to share text and graphics.

cybernetics Branch of learning that seeks to integrate the theories and studies of communication and control in machines and living organisms.

cyberphobia Fear of computers.

cyberpunk A science fiction hacker who plays around on future worldwide computer networks. Cyberpunks were first envisioned by William Gibson in his science fiction novel, *Necromancer*.

cyberspace A world in which computers and people coexist. Cyberspace is "where" you are when you're online with a computer, and when you put on a virtual reality headset. The term was coined by William Gibson in his science fiction novel, *Necromancer*.

cylinder As related to magnetic disks, a vertical column of tracks on a magnetic disk pack. The corresponding tracks on each surface of a disk pack.

daisywheel printer Printer that uses a metal or plastic disk with printed characters along its edge. The disk rotates until the required character is brought before a hammer that strikes it against a ribbon.

data Formalized representation of facts or concepts suitable for communication, interpretation, or processing by people or by automatic means. Raw material of information. Individual pieces of quantitative information, such a dollar sales of carpets, numbers of building permits issued, units of raw material on hand. Historically, data is a plural noun while datum is singular — a distinction now generally ignored in data processing terminology.

database A set of interrelated files that is created and managed by a database management system.

database administrator Person responsible for the creation of the information system database and, once it is established, for maintaining its security and developing procedures for its recovery from disaster.

database management system (DBMS) Collection of hardware and software that organizes and provides access to a database. The computer program provides the mechanisms needed to create a computerized database file, to add data to the file, to alter data in the file, to organize data within the file, to search for data in the file, and so forth. In other words, it manages data.

database server A network resource that stores one or more databases.

database software A computer program that helps you store, sort, print, and retrieve information. It allows you to work with a collection of data.

data bus A connection or circuit used to interconnect the CPU, the storage, and all of the input/output devices used in a computer system.

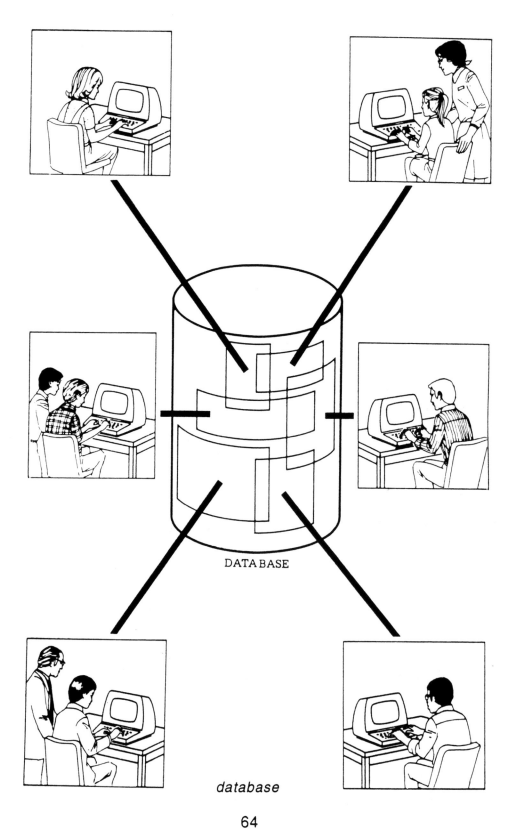

DATABASE

database

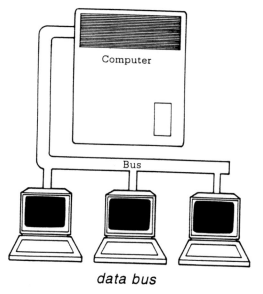

data bus

data collection Involves the gathering of information to be entered into a computer system.

data compression Technique that saves computer storage space by eliminating empty fields, gap redundancies, or unnecessary data to reduce the size or the length of records.

data entry (1) Process of converting data into a form suitable for entry into a computer system, such as by keying from a terminal onto magnetic disk or tape. (2) Process of entering data directly into a computer system.

data file A collection of data records.

Data General Corporation A minicomputer manufacturer founded in 1968 by Edson de Castro. A year later the company introduced the Nova, a popular minicomputer at the time. In following years the company produced several minicomputers for the academic, scientific, and OEM markets.

data processing (1) One or more operations performed on data to achieve a desired objective. (2) All functions of a computer center. (3) Operations performed by data processing equipment. (4) Operations performed on data to provide useful information to users.

data processing director The person in charge of developing and/or implementing the overall plan for transaction processing in an organization and for overseeing the activities of programmers, systems analysts, and operations personnel.

Satellite

Overseas factory

data structure   How data are organized in computer memory. Some data structures are arrays, files, lists and stacks.

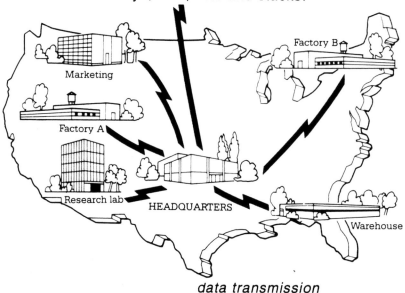

data transmission

data transmission   The sending of information from one location to another location.

data type   Programming languages allow data to be represented in a variety of ways. Some functions and operators will work on some data types but not on others, so it is necessary to keep them distinct. Data types include integer, fixed point, floating point, complex, logical, string and double precision. Each programming language uses a selection of data types.

daughter board   A printed circuit board that attaches either to a computer's main circuit board (the motherboard) or to an expansion board.

da Vinci, Leonardo (1452-1519)   A towering Renaissance figure of fifteenth-century Italy. Not only was he a great painter but also a genius who could bring an artist's discipline, training and insight to the pursuit of scientific achievement. He designed a calculator that had 13 decimal wheels and a carry mechanism. Nobody knows whether he ever made a model or whether later inventors knew about his design. His calculator model remained a mystery until the rediscovery in 1967 in Madrid, Spain of two bound volumes of his notebook materials.

Leonardo da Vinci

dBASE A relational database management system for IBM-compatible microcomputer systems. dBASE IV was introduced in 1988, a major upgrade of earlier versions.

DBMS An acronym for DataBase Management System, a program used for managing collections of information. The program allows items in a database to be organized, manipulated, and retrieved.

dealer One who sells for profit computer-related equipment, software, and services.

debug To detect, locate, and remove all mistakes in a computer program and any malfunctions in the computing system itself.

decryption Process of taking an encrypted message and reconstructing from it the original meaningful message, or plain text. Opposite of *encryption*.

dedicated Pertaining to programs, machines, or procedures that are designed or reserved for special use.

de facto standard A programming language, hardware product, design or program that has become so widely used and imitated that it has little competition but whose status has not officially been declared by a recognized standard establishing organization.

default Assumption made by a system or program when no specific choice is given by the program or the user. A choice that has been pre-set for you. You can override it or simply accept the setting which the manufacturer or developer has deemed most likely appropriate.

defragmentation A process in which all the files on a hard disk are rewritten so that all parts of each file are written to contiguous sectors. The reorganization of a file to eliminate fragmentation.

delete (1) To remove or eliminate. To erase data from a field or to eliminate a record from a file. (2) Method of erasing data.

delete key A keyboard key that erases the character above or to the right of the on-screen cursor.

delimiter Special character, often a comma or space, used to separate variable names or items in a list or to separate one string of characters from another, as in the separation of data items.

Dell Computer Corporation A manufacturer of IBM-compatible microcomputers that was founded in 1984 by Michael Dell in Austin, Texas. Dell provides a complete line of microcomputers from laptops to high-end machines.

Delphi Information Service A commercial online information network that was formed in 1982. In addition to its own package of services, Delphi is also connected to the Internet. See *Internet*.

demo A demonstration program designed to emulate some of the functions of an application program for advertising and marketing purposes.

demodulation In data communications, the process of retrieving an original signal from a modulated carrier wave. Used in data sets to make communications signals compatible with computer terminal signals. Counterpart to modulation.

demon dialer A program run from outside an organization's environment and control, usually by hackers, to find dial-up ports into computer systems. Such a program identifies numbers in a given range that connect to a computer.

density Number of characters that can be stored in a given physical space. Measures how close together data are recorded on a magnetic medium, usually in bytes per inch. As recording density increases, the capacity of a storage device increases. See *double density*.

descender Portion of lower-case letters (g, j, p, q, and y) that extends below the baseline of other characters.

design automation (DA) The technique of using a computer to automate portions of the design process and reduce human intervention.

desk accessory (DA) In a graphical user interface, helpful utilities (e.g., calculator, notepad, thesaurus, paint program, word processor, etc.) that you can open when you are in the middle of any program. Desk accessories are accessed by selecting them from a special pull-down menu. Desk accessories are conveniences that can be activated when needed and then either put away or moved to a small part of the display screen.

desktop (1) Screen display containing icons that represent programs, files or resources available to the user. (2) Small enough to fit on the top of an office desk, particularly a computer system.

desktop computer

desktop computer A computer that will fit on the top of a standard-sized office desk. Most personal computers and lap computers can be considered desktop computers. A desktop computer is equipped with sufficient internal memory and auxiliary storage to perform business computing tasks.

desktop publishing When printed pieces including words and pictures (ads, newsletters, magazines, brochures, books) are created almost entirely on a computer. Desktop publishing programs convert normal text into professional quality documents that can be printed on laser printers or imagesetters. The term "desktop publishing" was coined by Paul Brainerd, president of Aldus Corporation, the developer of PageMaker.

destination Device or address that receives the data during a data transfer operation.

detachable keyboard Keyboard not built into the same case as the video display or desk unit. Connects to the system with a cable and allows greater flexibility in positioning of the keyboard display — one result of *ergonomics*.

device driver A special section of computer code that translates the general commands from an operating system or user programs into the exact code a specific peripheral device needs. Often, device drivers for a few standard peripherals are built into the operating system, but others must be added in installation. For example: your printer needs a driver, your mouse needs a driver. Generally speaking, drivers come with the new hardware or as part of any major software package. Once installed, you can forget about them.

diagnostic (1) A message sent to the user by the computer system pinpointing errors in syntax or logic. (2) Diagnostics are often referred to as error messages.

dialog box Interactive message box. A temporary window on the screen that contains a set of choices whenever the executing program needs to collect information from the user.

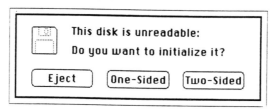

dialog box

Difference Engine A mechanical machine devised by Charles Babbage in 1822 to perform computations automatically and print their results. See *Babbage, Charles.*

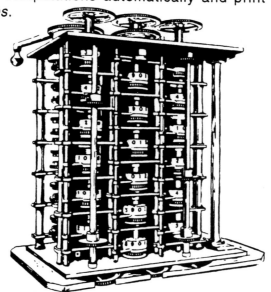

Difference Engine

Differential Analyzer An analog computational device built in 1930 by Vannevar Bush to solve differential equations. This large machine weighed 100 tons and used thousands of vacuum tubes. See *Bush, Vannevar.*

digit One of the symbols of a numbering system used to designate a quantity. The decimal system has ten digits, 0 through 9.

digital Using numbers to measure and show results. Most computers work with digital data in binary form.

digital computer

digital computer A computer that operates on discrete data. A device that performs arithmetic, logical, and comparative functions upon information represented in digital form and that operates under control of an internal program. Digital means that the computer uses data in the form of discrete numbers; for example, binary ones and zeros. Most computers used today (mainframes, minicomputers and microcomputers), are digital. Contrast with *analog computer*.

Digital Darkroom An image processing program from Silicon Beach Software that acts as a computerized darkroom to compose images. The program uses computer processing techniques to edit and enhance scanned images.

Digital Equipment Corporation (DEC) A major manufacturer of minicomputer systems, founded in 1957 by Kenneth Olsen. DEC pioneered the minicomputer business with its PDP computers in 1959. The popular PDP-8 was introduced in 1965, and the PDP-11 was introduced in 1970. In 1977, DEC announced the VAX series minicomputer systems and gained a strong foothold in commercial data processing. Over the years, DEC has been widely recognized for its reliable computer systems. See *Olsen, Kenneth*.

digital plotter A machine that can be controlled by a computer to draw pictures with an ink pen.

digitize (1) To register a visual image or real object in a format that can be processed by the computer. Digitized data are read into the system with graphics input devices. It includes scanning an image, tracing a picture on a graphics tablet or converting camera images into the computer. (2) To convert an analog signal (voltage or temperature) into a digital value.

digitizing Process of converting graphic representations, such as pictures and drawings, into digital data that can be processed by a computer system.

digitizing camera A camera coupled with a processor used for encoding highly detailed images such as pictures or three-dimensional objects into digital data.

digitizing tablet

digitizing tablet A graphic input device that allows the user to create images. It has a special stylus that can be used to draw or trace images, which are then converted to digital data that can be processed by the computer.

Dijkstra, Edsger W. (born 1930) A Dutchman who entered the programming profession in 1952, and three years later, decided to help make programming a respectable discipline in the years to come. The working vocabulary of programmers everywhere is studded with words originated or forcefully promulgated by Dijkstra — display, semaphore, deadly embrace, go-to-less programming, and structured programming. Dijkstra has had a strong influence on programming.

Edsger Dijkstra

dimmed command A command in a pull-down menu that is grayed-black. A dimmed command means that the choice is not currently available to you; perhaps because another function needs to be accomplished before that selection can be made.

dimmed icon A grayed-black icon indicates that the object it represents, such as a disk, or a folder, or document on a disk, has either been opened or been ejected from the disk drive.

dingbats Small graphical elements used for decorative purposes in a document. Some fonts, such as Zapf Dingbats, are designed to present sets of dingbats.

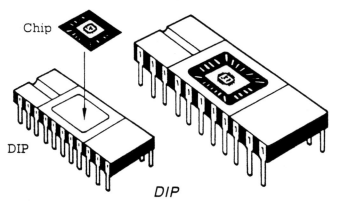

Chip

DIP

DIP

DIP Acronym for Dual Inline Package, a standard packaging and mounting device for integrated circuits.

DIP switch A miniature switch or a set of switches often used in computer equipment. DIP, or dual-inline package, means that the switch is the same size and shape as an integrated circuit.

directory (1) In a partition by software into several distinct files, a directory is maintained on a device to locate these files. (2) Index file containing the names and locations of all the files contained on a storage medium. (3) Major section of your hard disk drive. You can name as many directories as you like, and create subdirectories within them. As you create files, then, you will store the files in the directories.

direct voice input Spoken words that the computer can accept and process as data.

disclaimer Clause associated with many software products that states the vendor is not responsible for any business losses incurred due to the use of the product.

disk Magnetic device for storing information and programs accessible by a computer. Can be either a rigid platter (*hard disk*) or a sheet of flexible plastic (*floppy disk*). Disks have tracks where data is stored.

disk buffer Area of a computer's memory set aside to hold information not yet written to disk.

disk capacity The maximum number of megabytes of data that a disk can store.

disk cache An area of computer memory where data is temporarily stored on its way to or from a disk.

disk capacity The storage capacity of a hard or floppy disk, usually in kilobytes (KB), megabytes (MB), or gigabytes (GB).

disk compression utility A program which reduces the amount of space that files take up on a hard drive.

disk crash Condition of a disk unit that makes it unusable. Usually caused by contact between the read/write head of the disk drive and the surface of the disk.

disk directory A catalog. This is the computer's own record of where each file or program is stored on the disk. The directory usually takes up a few tracks at the beginning of a disk.

disk drive Device that reads data from a magnetic disk and copies it into the computer's memory so it can be used by the computer, and that writes data from the computer's memory onto a disk so it can be stored. See *floppy disk* and *hard disk*.

diskette A single magnetic disk on which data is recorded as magnetic spots. Available in both 3.5-inch format and 5.25-inch format.

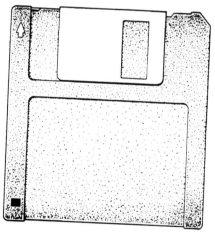

diskette

disk operating system (DOS) A collection of software stored on disk that controls the operation of the computer system. A computer cannot function unless it has access to its own operating system. Typically, it keeps track of files, saves and retrieves files, allocates storage space, and manages other control functions associated with disk storage.

disk utility A software program that helps you recover erased or damaged files, or a damaged disk.

74

display (1) Physical representation of data, as on a screen or display. (2) Lights or indicators on computer consoles. (3) Process of creating a visual representative of graphic data on an output device.

display resolution The number of pixels the monitor can use to display a image. The higher the resolution, the sharper the image quality. In high resolution, a computer can light up a large number of small pixels and make very detailed pictures. In low resolution, the pictures a computer can make are not very detailed because the pixels are quite large and there are fewer of them than in high resolution

display unit A device that presents computer output in visual form.

distributed data processing (DDP) system A processing system that uses a mainframe computer for database storage and for large-scale processing combined with minicomputers or personal computers for local processing.

dithering The creation of additional colors or shades of gray to create special effects or to make "hard edges" softer. Dithering takes advantage of the eye's tendency to blur spots of different colors by averaging their effects and merging them into a single perceived shade or color. Dithering is used to add realism to computer graphics, and to create a wide variety of patterns for use as backgrounds, fills and shading.

document (1) A file containing a text or drawing to be printed. (2) A printed form containing text and/or illustrations.

documentation (1) During systems analysis and subsequent programming, the preparation of documents that describe such things as the system, the programs prepared, and the changes made at later dates. See *program development cycle*. (2) Internal documentation in the form of comments or remarks.

document reader An input device that reads printed data into a computer system. The data is interpreted by an optical character recognition program as text.

DOS Operating system for IBM-compatible microcomputers. DOS is available in both generic MS-DOS and IBM-specific PC DOS versions. DOS is an acronym for Disk Operating System.

dot matrix printer Printer that creates text characters and graphs with a series of closely spaced dots. Uses tiny hammers to strike a needle

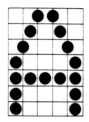

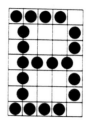

dot matrix printer

mechanism against the paper at precise moments as the print head moves across the page. Some produce dot patterns fine enough to approach the print quality of a typewriter. See *laser printer.*

dot pitch   The spacing between the pixels on a monitor.

dots per inch   (1) A linear measure of the number of dots a printer can print in an inch. For example, a 600 dpi laser printer can print up to 600 dots for each horizontal or vertical inch on the paper. (2) A measure of screen resolution that counts the dots that the device can produce per linear inch.

double-click   Method to invoke a command by using the mouse button. The pointer or cursor is placed in the correct position on a display screen and the mouse button is pressed twice in rapid succession. A double-click is used to open a file, disk or folder.

double density   Having twice the storage capacity of a normal disk or tape. Ability to store twice as much data in a given area on a disk or tape as *single density.*

double precision   The use of two computer words to express larger numbers than could fit into one.

double-sided disk   Magnetic disk capable of storing information on both of its surfaces.

Dow Jones News/Retrieval Service   An online financial information service from Dow Jones, the publisher of the Wall Street Journal.

down   Said of a computer that is not running. It may be shut down for maintenance, there may be a hardware problem, or the operating system may not be working properly.

download   (1) Process of transferring data (files) from a large computer to a smaller one. (2) To transfer information to a laser printer from a computer. Opposite of *upload*.

downtime   The time a computer is not operating due to a hardware or software failure.

dpi   See *dots per inch*.

draft quality   Measure of quality for printed output. Usually refers to the result of top-speed printing and therefore not the most precisely defined or fully filled-in characters. Considered acceptable for working copies but not final work.

drag   Action of moving the mouse while holding the button down; used to move or manipulate objects on a computer's display screen.

drag

DRAM   Short for dynamic memory, meaning a type of memory chip that keeps its contents only if supplied with regular clock pulses and a chance to periodically refresh the data internally. DRAM is far less expensive than static RAM (which needs no refreshing) and is the type found in most personal computers.

draw program A program for creating and manipulating object-oriented graphics, as opposed to creating and manipulating pixel images. For example, in a drawing program the user can manipulate an element such as a triangle, or a block of text as an independent object simply by selecting the object and moving it.

drive See *disk drive*.

drop cap An initial letter of a chapter or paragraph enlarged and positioned so that the top of the character is even with the top of the first line and the rest of the character descends into the second and subsequent lines.

drop-down menu A type of menu that drops from the menu bar when requested and remains open without further action until the user closes it or chooses a menu item. Same as *pull-down menu*.

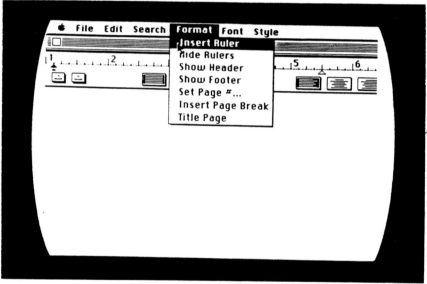

drop down menu

drop shadow A shadow placed behind an image, slightly off-set horizontally and vertically, that creates the illusion that the topmost image has been lifted off the surface of the page. Drop shadow is very difficult to draw manually, but can be generated by computer graphics instantly. The dropshadow is a feature found in many paint programs.

dumb terminal A display terminal without processing capability.

dumping Copying all or part of the contents of a storage unit, usually from the computer's internal storage, into an auxiliary storage unit or onto a printer.

duplex printing Printing a document on both sides of the sheet, so that the verso (left) and recto (right) pages face each other after the document is bound.

Dvorak keyboard Keyboard arrangement designed by August Dvorak in the 1930s. Provides increased speed and comfort and reduces the rate of errors by placing the most frequently used letters in the center for use by the strongest fingers. See *Maltron keyboard* and *QWERTY keyboard*.

Dvorak keyboard

dynamic RAM (DRAM) The most common type of computer memory; the computer must refresh DRAM at frequent intervals. Contrast with static RAM, which is usually faster and does not require refresh circuitry.

EBCDIC Acronym for Extended Binary Coded Decimal Interchange Code, an 8-bit code used to represent data in large IBM mainframes. EBCDIC can represent up to 256 distinct characters and is the principal code used in many of the current computers.

echo (1) In data communications, the return of a transmitted signal to its source, with a delay that indicates the signal is a reflection rather than the original. (2) In computer graphics, to provide visual feedback to the designer during graphic input to the system.

Eckert, J. Presper (1919-1995)   Coinventor of ENIAC. Collaborated with John Mauchly at the Moore School of Electrical Engineering, University of Pennsylvania, on developing the Electronic Numerical Integrator And Computer for Army Ordnance between 1943 and 1946. This was the first large-scale, all-electronic digital computer. Its development launched the computer industry as we know it today. See *ENIAC* and *Mauchly, John.*

J. Presper Eckert

edge connector The part of an adapter board that plugs into an expansion slot.

edit To modify, refine, or update an emerging design or text on a computer system.

EDSAC An acronym for Electronic Delay Storage Automatic Calculator. EDSAC was the world's first stored program computer and was completed in Great Britain in 1949.

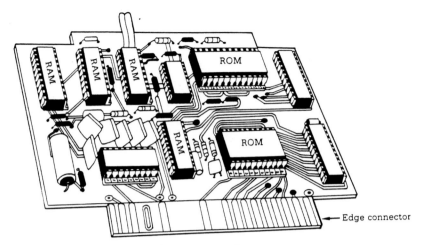

edge connector

EDVAC An acronym for Electronic Discrete Variable Automatic Calculator. Completed in 1950, EDVAC was the first stored program computer built in the United States.

EGA Acronym for Enhanced Graphics Adapter, a video display adapter introduced by IBM in 1984. Video display standard for IBM-compatible microcomputers featuring 640- by 350-pixel resolution. EGA can display no more than 16 colors at once. EGA has been superseded by VGA.

EISA See *extended industry standard architecture*.

electronic Computer technology involves the selective use and combination of electronic devices. In these devices, electrical current can be allowed to flow or can be halted by electronic switches working at very high speed.

electronic bulletin board Computer system that maintains a list of messages so people can call up (with their computer systems) and either post a message or read those already there.

electronic cottage Concept of permitting workers to remain at home to perform work, using computer terminals connected to a central office.

electronic funds transfer A cashless method of paying for goods or services. The payment for something is accomplished by communications between computers rather than by using cash or checks.

electronic mail Process of sending, receiving, storing, and forwarding messages in digital form over telecommunication facilities. Also called *E-mail*.

electronic pen A pen-like device which is commonly used in conjunction with a display terminal. It is sometimes called a *light pen*.

electronic publishing (1) Technology encompassing a variety of activities that contain or convey information with a high editorial and value-added content in a form other than print. Includes educational software disks, CD-ROM, online databases, electronic mail, videotext, teletext, videotape cassettes, and videodisks. (2) Use of a personal computer, special software, and a laser printer to produce very high-quality documents that combine text and graphics. Also called *desktop publishing*.

electronic spreadsheet Computer program that turns a computer terminal into a huge ledger sheet. Allows large columns and rows of numbers to change according to parameters determined by the user. A whole range of numbers can be changed when a single entry is varied, allowing complex projections and numerical forecasts to be performed without tedious manual calculations.

```
                  DEPRECIATION TABLE
=================================================

Description          :        Computer
Original Cost        $        10000.00      Dollars
Salvage Value        $         2000.00      Dollars
Length of Term       :               7      Years
Rate of Depreciation           200.00      Per Cent
-------------------------------------------------
             Schedule of Remaining Value
-------------------------------------------------
Year        Current        Amount of          Value
             Value        Depreciation     Remaining
..................................................
  1         10000.00        2857.14          7142.86
  2          7142.86        2040.82          5102.04
  3          5102.04        1457.73          3644.31
  4          3644.31        1041.23          2603.08
  5          2603.08         603.08          2000.00
  6          2000.00           0.00          2000.00
  7          2000.00           0.00          2000.00
-------------------------------------------------
Average Amount of Depreciation        $      1142.86
-------------------------------------------------
```

electronic spreadsheet

E-mail Abbreviation for electronic mail, a communications service for computer users wherein textual messages are sent to a central computer system, or electronic "mailbox," and later retrieved by the addressee. E-mail usually refers to private messages. Bulletin board usually refers to public messages.

embedded object (1) One or more codes inserted into a document that do not print but direct the application program or printer to control printing and change formats. (2) Low-level assembly level instructions that are inserted within a program written in a high-level language. Embedded code is used to make a program more efficient or to produce a capability not available in the high-level language. (3) A document or part of a document that has been embedded in another document.

embedded systems Preprogrammed microprocessors built into another device, such as an automobile, a camera, or a copy machine.

em dash A unit of measure equal to the width of the capital M in a particular font.

emulate (1) To imitate one hardware system with another, by means of an electronic attachment, such that the imitating system accepts the same data, executes the same programs, and achieves the same results as the imitated system. (2) To have a program simulate the function of another software or hardware product. Printers often have emulation options so that you can specify a brand name in configuration or setup, even though you don't have that brand.

en dash One half the width of the *em dash*.

encapsulated PostScript (EPS) A file format developed to facilitate the exchange of PostScript graphics files between applications. Like all PostScript files, EPS files are resolution independent and can be printed by a PostScript printer.

encryption The process of coding, or encrypting, any data, in which a specific code or key is required to restore the original data. The process of encoding communications data. Opposite of *decryption*.

end user Person who buys and uses computer software or who has contact with computers. A user of a computer.

enhanced graphics adapter (EGA) A computer graphics board that allows presentation of color graphics and text.

enhanced keyboard A standard keyboard for newer IBM personal computers. It has become the de facto standard for most IBM-compatible keyboards.

ENIAC Acronym for Electronic Numerical Integrator And Calculator, the first large-scale, all-electronic digital computer. Built by John Mauchly and J. Presper Eckert at the Moore School of Electrical Engineering, University of Pennsylvania, in 1946. Occupied 1500 sq. ft., weighed about 30 tons, contained approximately 18,000 vacuum tubes, and required 130 kw of

ENIAC

power. The computing elements consisted of many components with about one million hand-soldered connections. The input/output system was modified IBM card readers and punches. ENIAC could perform 5000 additions per second, relatively slow by today's standards. But in 1946, the only machine that could even compete with it was the ASCC relay calculator, which performed only 10 additions per second. ENIAC made all relay calculators obsolete. It could perform several additions, a multiplication, and a square root in parallel, as well as solve several independent problems at the same time. ENIAC was so successful that it marked the end of the pioneer stage of automatic computer development. After nine years of operation, ENIAC was retired from service in 1955. See *Eckert, J. Presper* and *Mauchly, John.*

ENTER key Special key on some keyboards that means "execute a command." Same as RETURN key on some keyboards.

entry In an electronic spreadsheet, the value or information contained within a specific cell.

environment In a computing context, this is more likely to refer to the mode of operation, such as a network environment, than to physical conditions of temperature, humidity, and so forth. With respect to personal computers, everything surrounding the PC, including peripherals and software.

EPS Acronym for Encapsulated PostScript. A directly printable PostScript file; the output of a PostScript compatible printer driver captured in a file instead of being sent to a printer.

Epson A popular make of dot-matrix printers.

erasable optical disk An optical disk on which data can be stored, moved, changed, and erased, just as on magnetic media. Erasable drives perform much like large, interchangeable hard disks. Erasable drives use two lasers rather than one; one laser melts the surface of the media to an amorphous state, effectively erasing any information stored there — the other laser writes or reads information.

erase To remove data from storage without replacing it.

ergonomics Study of the physical relationships between people and their work environment. Adapting machines to the convenience of operators, with the general aim of maximum efficiency and physical well being. Numeric keypads on standard keyboards, detachable keyboards, and tilting display screens are tangible results. The word comes from ergo (work) and nomics (law or management).

ergonomics

error Any deviation of a computed or a measured quantity from the theoretically correct or true value.

error message Printed or displayed statement indicating the computer has detected a mistake or malfunction.

ESCAPE key Standard control key available on most computer keyboards. Used to take control of the computer away from a program, to escape from a specific program, or to stop a program. Abbreviated ESC.

Ethernet A local area network standard capable of linking up to 1024 nodes in a bus network.

even footer In word processing, a footer that appears on even-numbered pages.

even header In word processing, a header that appears on even-numbered pages.

eWorld An Apple Computer Inc. on-line computer service. Users can get news, information and other services from about 100 concerns.

Excel See *Microsoft Excel*.

execute (1) To run a program on a computer. (2) To carry out the instructions in an algorithm or program.

Exemplar Scalable Parallel Processor A supercomputer introduced by Convex Computer in 1994. It used as many as 128 RISC processors, with up to 32 gigabytes of memory, to attain up to 25-gigaflops performance.

expandability Ability to increase the capability of a computer system by adding modules or devices.

expansion card A circuit board that plugs into a computer and gives it additional specialized functions (e.g. enhanced graphics, expanded memory, modem).

expansion slot A receptacle inside a computer which is used to plug in printed circuit boards. The number of expansion slots determines the amount of future expansion that is possible within the existing computer system.

expert system An artificial intelligence application that uses a knowledge base of human expertise to aid in solving problems.

exploded pie graph A pie graph in which one or more of the slices has been offset slightly from the others.

exploded view Illustration of a solid construction showing its parts separately, but in positions that indicate their relationships to the whole.

export To transfer information from one system or program to another. Opposite of *import*.

expression (1) General term for numerals, numerals with signs of operation, variables, and combinations of these. See arithmetic expression. (2) Any arithmetic formula coded in a programming language.

extended filename A filename that includes the letter of the disk, the directory, the filename, and the file extension all in its name.

extended industry standard architecture (EISA) A next generation outgrowth of the popular ISA (Industry Standard Architecture). It incorporates features of ISA yet is designed to be faster and more versatile.

extended memory Additional memory chips added to the computer.

extension (1) Additional feature added to a programming language or computer system. Feature beyond what is regularly available in the standard. (2) In reference to a filename that serves to extend or clarify its meaning.

external CD-ROM An optical disk equipped with its own case, cables, and power supply.

external drive A disk drive that sits in its own case, rather than being mounted in the chassis of the main computer. Often, external drives include their own power supply.

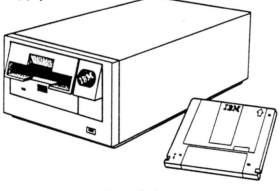

external drive

external memory A memory unit equipped with its own case, cables and power supply. Can be extra RAM, ROM, hard disk or floppy disk.

eye control computer In 1986, Analytics Inc. developed a prototype computer that obeys sound and the eye. It uses an infrared beam to record eye movements. The user stares at a point on the screen, then gives a command to a microcomputer and the machine carries it out immediately. This system could facilitate the control of robots or the selection of components on an assembly line.

facsimile The use of computer technology to send digitized text graphics and charts from one facsimile machine to another. Abbreviated FAX.

family (1) In computer science, a compatible series of computers, i.e., Macintosh Classic, Macintosh LC, and Macintosh IIsi all constitute a family of microcomputers. (2) In desktop publishing, a family of type, i.e., Helvetica, *Helvetica Italic*, **Helvetica Bold**, and ***Helvetica Bold Italic*** all constitute a family of type.

fan The cooling mechanism built into computer cabinets, laser printers and other devices to prevent malfunction due to heat buildup.

fanfold paper One long continuous sheet of paper perforated at regular intervals to mark page boundaries and folded fan-style into a stack. Fanfold paper is available with vertical perforations, so the sprocket hole strip can be removed. The paper can be divided on the perforations thus enabling the paper to be separated into sheets.

fatal error An error in program execution that causes the program to abort; no hope of recovery without rebooting.

fault A condition that causes a part of the computer system not to work properly.

fault tolerance The ability to resist and recover from breakdowns and errors.

fax The use of computer technology to send digitized text, graphics, and charts from one facsimile machine to another. Facsimile.

feathering The process of adding an even amount of space between each line on a page or column to force vertical justification.

feature Something special accomplished in a program or hardware device, such as the ability of a paint program to create animation cells, or a word processing program to check the spelling of words.

feed (1) To supply data or materials to any device. (2) Mechanical process whereby lengthy materials — such as magnetic tape, line printer paper, and printer ribbon — are moved along the required operating position. (3) To insert disks into a disk drive.

feedback A method of controlling a process by measuring its own effect on the environment.

Felt, Dorr Eugene (1862-1930) Co-founder of Felt & Tarrant Manufacturing Company, inventor of the internationally famous "Comptometer," was granted his basic patent in 1887, and that same year his company produced its first commercial machines, eight of them, all hand built. Serious manufacturing and sale of the Comptometer began in 1888. Felt was also the inventory of the first practical recording-adding machine. The first of these machines, called the "Comptograph," was sold in 1889.

Dorr Felt

female connector Recessed portion of a connecting device into which another part fits. Contrast with *male connector*.

fetch To locate an item of data in storage (floppy disk, hard disk, optical disk) and bring it into the main memory (RAM) for processing.

fiber optic cable A cable that carries light rather than electrical energy. It is made of a thin fiber of glass. Large amounts of data can be carried by a single fiber optic cable.

FidoNet A set of data exchange standards and procedures that tie together over 25,000 bulletin board systems. FidoNet lets people from all over the world communicate easily.

field Single piece of information, the smallest unit normally manipulated by a database management system. In a personnel file, the person's name and age would be separate fields. A record is made up of one or more fields.

field engineer The service technician who fixes computers and related equipment.

fifth-generation computer The next generation of computers. A term describing new forms of computer systems involving artificial intelligence, natural language, and expert systems. Fifth-generation computer systems are expected to appear in the late 1990s and will represent the next quantum leap in computer technology.

file A collection of related information in the system which may be accessed by a unique name. May be stored on a disk, tape, or other storage media.

file compression See *compression*.

file deletion Removing the file name from the directory.

file fragmentation A condition in which there are many scattered areas of storage that are too small to be used productively.

file locking Protects shared files by allowing only one user at a time to make changes.

file maintenance Updating of a file to reflect the effects of nonperiodic changes by adding, altering, or deleting data.

file management Creation and maintenance of files by means of computer.

filename Alphanumeric characters used to identify a particular file.

file protection Technique or device used to prevent accidental erasure of data from a file.

file recovery A broad term used to describe any method for getting back a file that's been lost or damaged.

file server The central repository of shared files and applications in a computer network.

fill (1) To place a pattern or color in a defined region. (2) A color or pattern occupying a region.

film recorder An output device that takes a 35 mm slide picture from a graphics file which has been created using a graphics program. Widely used in producing presentation-quality hardcopy. Film recorders offer both high resolution (up to 2000 dots per inch) and a true color reproduction capability (up to 6 million simultaneous colors). Lines show perfectly smooth edges, and colors blend imperceptibly in film recorder images.

filter A software function that modifies an image by altering the gray values of certain pixels.

finder A system program that provides the "desktop" metaphor you encounter when a Macintosh microcomputer is booted up. The finder presents icons (little pictures) depicting applications, documents, file folders, and a garbage can that can be used to discard unwanted files. This highly visual interface program keeps the user from having to type commands directly to the operating system.

firmware Software that has been copied on integrated circuits, usually ROMs. Since it is on ROM, which cannot be altered, it is neither completely soft nor hard and therefore referred to as firm.

first generation computers First commercially available computers, introduced with UNIVAC 1 in 1951 and terminated with the development of fully transistorized computers in 1959. Characterized by their use of vacuum tubes, they are now museum pieces.

fixed disk Same as *hard disk*.

flatbed plotter Digital plotter using plotting heads that move over a flat surface in both vertical and horizontal directions. The size of the bed determines the maximum size sheet of paper that can be drawn. A pair of arms attached to a trolley and controlled by a computer can place the trolley at any part of the paper. A pen attached to the trolley can be raised or lowered to contact the paper. Then, under computer control, this device can draw pictures. If several pens of different colors can be controlled, then pictures can be drawn in color.

flatbed scanner A scanner with a glass surface upon which you place material to be scanned. Because the original never moves during the scanning process, flatbeds produce more precise results than sheetfed scanners. The scanner can transform a full-page (8.5- by 11-inch) graphic or page of text into a digitized file.

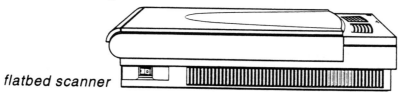

flatbed scanner

flicker Undesirable, unsteady lighting of a display due to inadequate refresh rate and/or fast persistence. Occurs whenever the refresh speed is not fast enough to compensate for natural luminance delay on the screen.

floating-point unit A special processor (called a math coprocessor) section of a processor designed specifically to handle complex math calculations quickly.

floppy disk Floppy disks are a form of computer storage medium consisting of a thin flexible disk covered with magnetic oxide held inside a protective sleeve within which it can be rotated. They are lightweight, cheap and portable. Floppy disks, universally used on microcomputers, were invented in 1950 at the Imperial University in Tokyo by Yoshiro Nakamats, an inventor who boasts of having 2,360 patents for objects as diverse as golf clubs and loudspeakers. He granted the sales license for the disk to the IBM Corporation.

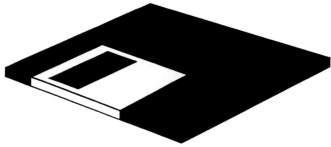

floppy disk

FLOPS Abbreviation for FLoating point Operations Per Second. A computer's capacity for high-speed number processing is measured in FLOPS or MFLOPS (Million FLOPS).

floptical disk A removable optical disk with a 3.5 inch diameter. Floptical disk drives are used to read and write information on these small disks. A floptical disk can store up to 25 megabytes of information.

flow (1) In a page layout program, importing text into a specified area. (2) In a graphics program or page layout program, wrapping text around a graphic object on the same page. (3) In a program, the progression from one instruction to the next.

flowchart Diagram that uses symbols and interconnecting lines to show (1) the logic and sequence of specific program operations (program flowchart), or (2) a system of processing to achieve objectives (system flowchart).

flush left Pertaining to text that is aligned to the left margin but need not be aligned to the right margin.

flush right Pertaining to text that is aligned to the right margin but need not be aligned to the left margin.

FOCUS An acronym for Federation On Computing in the U.S.; the U.S. representative of IFIP. See *IFIP*.

folder A subdirectory on the Macintosh computer.

folio A page number.

font A complete assortment or set of all the characters (letters, numbers, punctuation and symbols) of a particular typeface, all of one size and style (e.g., 12 pt. Bookman, 18 pt. Helvetica, 36 pt. Cooper Black, 8 pt. Times Roman). Two types of fonts exist: bit-mapped fonts and outline fonts. Each comes in two versions, screen fonts and printer fonts.

font cartridge A set of fonts for one or more typefaces contained in a module that plugs into a laser printer slot. The fonts are stored in a ROM chip within the cartridge.

font family A set of fonts in several sizes and weights that share the same typeface.

font groups Fonts are often divided into three groups: Serif, Sans Serif, and Display. Type styles in the Serif group have additional strokes (serifs) at the top and bottom of each letter. Type styles in the Sans Serif group do not have serifs. Display (or decorative) type styles can be either Serif or Sans Serif. Type styles in this group are used when you want to create a dramatic effect in headings, logos, and product names. They are rarely used in long passages of text since they are typically difficult to read.

font smoothing In laser printers, the reduction of aliasing and other distortions when graphics or text are printed.

footer Information printed at the bottom of a page, such as page numbers.

footnote In a page layout or word processing program, a note positioned at the bottom of the page.

footprint The surface area occupied by a computer or peripheral. A small computer is said to have a small footprint. A machine with a large footprint may need a desk to itself.

forecasting A process that uses currently available information to predict future occurrences.

foreground processing Automatic execution of computer programs that have been designed to preempt the use of computing facilities. Contrast with *background processing*.

format (1) Specific arrangement of data. (2) Programming associated with setting up text arrangements for output. (3) Preparing a floppy disk for use so that the operating system can write information on it. Formatting erases any previous information there. (4) A pattern for the display, storage, or printing of data.

formula Rule expressed as an equation; for example, $C = 2\pi r$ is the formula for finding the circumference of a circle.

Forrester, Jay (born 1918) Leader in the area of system dynamics; developed magnetic core, an internal memory used in most computers between 1951 and 1964. Headed the team of people at M.I.T. who built the Whirlwind computer, perhaps the most influential of the early computers in terms of today's commercial machines. Both magnetic core memory and the parallel synchronous method for handling information inside the machine were first developed by Whirlwind's designers. After Whirlwind, Forrester went on to tackle the Semi-Automatic Ground Environment (SAGE), the sophisticated U.S. air defense system. In operation from 1958 until 1983, SAGE was built under Forrester's leadership.

Jay Forrester

FORTRAN Acronym for FORmula TRANslation, a scientific programming language used by many businesses and organizations in the past to develop computer software.

fourth-generation computers A computer that is made up almost entirely of chips with limited amounts of discrete components. Fourth-generation computers are currently being manufactured and sold.

fourth-generation language A user-oriented language that makes it possible to develop programs with fewer commands than those needed for older procedural languages. A nonprocedural language. Also called a 4GL language.

fractal A complex geometric shape that has an infinite number and variety of corners, twists, and curves. These shapes are used to study and simulate natural phenomena, such as atmospheric turbulence, geographical landscapes, cloud formations, and the distribution of stellar systems throughout the universe. In the simplest of terms, fractals imitate nature. The term fractal was invented by Benoit Mandelbrot. See *Mandelbrot, Benoit.*

fractal

fragmentation The condition of having different parts of the same file scattered throughout a disk.

Frankston, Bob When Daniel Bricklin got the idea for an electronic spreadsheet, he depended on Frankston to create a workable version of the program. Frankston developed a version of the program from Bricklin's prototype design. The two worked together until they completed the first electronic spreadsheet, VisiCalc, in 1979. By early 1983 approximately 400,000 copies of VisiCalc were in consumer hands. See *Bricklin, Daniel* and *VisiCalc.*

Bob Frankston

freeware Software provided by a vendor at no charge. Freeware developers often retain all rights to their software thus preventing users from copying it or distributing it further.

full duplex Duplex refers to a modem that can both send and receive data between computers. Full duplex means it is capable of sending and receiving at the same time. See *half duplex.*

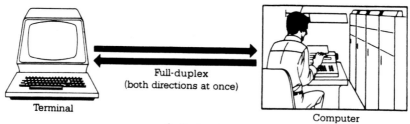

Full-duplex
(both directions at once)

Terminal

Computer

full duplex

full page display A monitor that allows viewing an entire page (8.5 in. x 11 in. vertical page) at actual size. Makes for greater flexibility and ease in desktop publishing or word processing applications.

full page display

function keys Specially designed keys that, when pressed, initiates some function on a computer keyboard, or graphics terminal. Most software assign function keys (F1, F2, etc.) for common tasks, but not universally. For example, in one word processor, F4 might mean "save file," while in a different word processor, F4 might mean "increase size of character." These special keys are programmed to execute commonly used commands.

function keys

fuzzy logic Method of handling imprecision or uncertainty that attaches various measures of credibility to propositions. A form of logic used in some expert systems and other artificial intelligence applications.

gallium arsenide Crystalline material used as a substitute for silicon in chip making. Superior to silicon but far more costly. It is several times faster than silicon.

gamut In computer graphics, the range of colors that can be displayed on a color monitor.

Garbage In-Garbage Out Invalid data entered into the computer produces invalid output.

Gates, William H. (born 1955) Bill Gates and his school friend, Paul Allen, created Microsoft BASIC for the microcomputer. Gates and Allen founded Microsoft Corporation in 1975. Microsoft Corporation, under the guidance of Gates has become the largest software development company in the world. A few of the products are MS-DOS, Microsoft Windows, Microsoft Word, Microsoft Works, GW-BASIC, as well as many other software systems. Bill Gates has built Microsoft Corporation into a software powerhouse. See *Microsoft Corporation.*

William Gates

gateway A device that connects two networks that use different communications protocols.

generation A level of mainframe computer development. The first generation of computers used vacuum tubes, the second generation used transistors, the third generation used early types of integrated circuits, the fourth generation uses large scale integrated circuits. The next generation of computers, the fifth generation, will represent the next quantum leap in computer technology.

GEnie An online information service, developed by the General Electric Company, that offers stock quotes, E-mail via Internet, home shopping, bulletin board and news services.

germanium Chemical element (atomic number 32) used in the manufacture of chips. In its pure state, germanium is an insulator. When small amounts of certain impurities, called dopants, are added, it becomes a semiconductor.

ghost A faint second image that appears close to the primary image on a display or printout.

ghost icon An outline of an icon or window used to show the current position of the icon or window as it is being dragged to a new location on the desktop.

GIF A graphics format often used for pictures that are transmitted by modem. Especially popular with computer bulletin boards and information services such as CompuServe. Acronym for *Graphic Interchange Format.*

giga A prefix indicating one billion.

gigabyte Specifically, 1,073,741,824 bytes. More loosely, one billion bytes, one million kilobytes, or one thousand megabytes. Abbreviated GB.

GIGO Acronym for Garbage In-Garbage Out, a term used to describe the data into and out of a computer system. If the input data is bad (Garbage In), then the output data will also be bad (Garbage Out).

glare Reflection from the surface of a display screen.

glitch Popular term for a temporary or random error, problem or malfunction in hardware, such as a malfunction caused by a power surge.

global (1) General term implying a great breadth of scope, as contrasted with local. (2) Pertaining to a variable whose name is accessible by a main program and all its subroutines. (3) Any computer operation applied to a broad set of data.

Gopher A menu-driven program that helps you locate and retrieve information on the Internet.

gppm Acronym for graphics pages per minute, the speed at which a laser printer can print pages of graphics images.

grabber (1) A device for capturing data, i.e., a video digitizer. (2) A computer program that takes a "snapshot" of the currently displayed screen image by transferring a portion of video memory to a file on disk. (3) Fixture on the end of a test equipment lead wire with a spring-actuated hook and claw designed to connect the measuring instrument to a pin of an integrated circuit, socket, transistor, and so forth.

grabber hand In graphics programs, an on-screen image of a hand that you can position with the mouse to move selected units of graphics or text from place to place on-screen.

grammar checker A program that checks for subject-verb disagreement, awkward phrases, wordiness, incomplete sentences and other grammar problems.

grandparent The oldest backup file in a group of related files.

graph A pictorial representation of information.

graphical user interface (GUI) A type of display format that enables the user to choose commands, start programs and see lists of files and other options by pointing to pictorial representations (icons) and lists of menu items on the screen. Graphical user interfaces are used on the Apple Macintosh microcomputer, by the Microsoft Windows, and Presentation Manager (OS/2) programs for IBM-compatible microcomputers, and other systems.

graphics Any computer-generated picture produced on a screen, paper, or film. Graphics range from simple line or bar graphs to colorful and detailed images. All computers have some amount of graphics capability, but today most feature high-resolution graphics in which the detail of the diagrams can be considerably finer than was possible in early systems. Modern microcomputers feature high-resolution graphics in color, and printed pictures can also be produced in color.

graphics

graphics accelerator An expansion board that includes a graphics coprocessor. The coprocessor is a microprocessor specially designed for fast graphics processing. Graphics accelerations calculate pixel values, and write them into the frame buffer, freeing up the central processing unit for other operations.

graphics adapters CGA-EGA-VGA adapters that must be matched with compatible monitors. Note the alphabetical order — it happens to match their order of age and sophistication: CGA was first, EGA was the new standard for a long while. VGA is now the popular standard for color presentations. VGA has higher resolution modes, and sharper text and image quality.

graphics coprocessor A special microprocessor chip, mounted on some video adaptors, that can generate graphical images, thereby freeing the computer for other work.

graphics program A computer program that aids computer users in producing computer generated images. Pictures can be entered into the computer using input devices such as mice, graphics tablets or light pens, and existing pictures on paper can be scanned into the computer using digitized scanners. Once stored in the computers memory pictures can be manipulated in a variety of ways and printed on paper, display screen or film.

graphics tablet

graphics tablet Input device that converts graphic and pictorial data into binary inputs for use in a computer. Provides an efficient method of converting object shapes into computer-storable information. Utilizes a flat tablet and a stylus for graphic input.

gray scale In computer graphics, a series of shades from white to black.

gray scale monitor A monitor capable of displaying a full range of shades from white to black on the display screen.

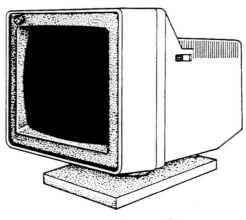

gray scale monitor

Greeking The use of random letters or marks to show the overall appearance of a printed page without showing the actual text.

grid Network of uniformly spaced points or crosshatched lines displayed on a visual display screen or digitizer and used for exactly locating a position, inputting components to assist in the creation of a design layout, or constructing precise diagrams.

groupware Software that is designed for use in a network and serve a group of users that work on a related project.

GUI See *graphical user interface.*

gutter (1) The margin at the binding edge of a page. (2) White space between a multiple-column page layout.

GW-BASIC A version of the BASIC programming language for MS-DOS computers; developed by Microsoft Corporation. GW-BASIC is nearly identical to the BASIC interpreter distributed with IBM personal computers and was included with older versions of DOS (before Version 5.0).

hacker (1) A skilled computer enthusiast who works alone and is obsessed with learning about programming and exploring the capabilities of computer systems. (2) A person who gains access to a computer system without authorization.

half duplex Refers to data communications between computers, in which the data can flow in only one direction at a time. See *full duplex*.

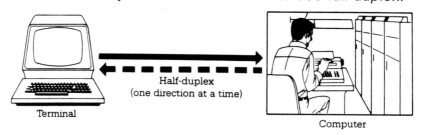

Half-duplex
(one direction at a time)

Terminal

Computer

half duplex

half-height drive A disk drive that occupies only half the vertical space of earlier disk drives.

halftone A continuous-tone image, e.g., a photograph, shot through a screen and reproduced as an array of tiny dots. A halftone is a printed reproduction of these tiny dots which the naked eye sees as various tones of gray shading into one another. Several page layout and image processing programs can output halftone images.

hand-held scanner An optical scanner that is operated by manually running a scanning head over an image. Small rollers on the bottom of the scanning head serve to guide the hand movement.

handle (1) In computer graphics, a small square associated with a graphical object that can be used to move or reshape the image. (2) A number that can be used to uniquely identify an object. (3) In programming, a pointer to a

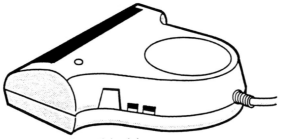

hand held scanner

pointer. In other words, a variable that contains the address of another variable, which in turn contains the address of yet another variable.

handshaking Procedures and standards (protocol) used by two computers or a computer and a peripheral device to establish communication.

hanging indent A paragraphing style with a full-measure first line and indented succeeding lines (called turnover lines).

hardcopy Computer output onto a tangible substrate, such as paper or film.

hard disk Fast auxiliary storage device either mounted in its own case or permanently mounted inside a computer. A single hard disk has storage capacity of several million characters or bytes of information. This storage media makes computers usable in the real world. Contrast with *floppy disk.*

hard hyphen Hyphen required by spelling and always printed, such as in CD-ROM, or high-level. Contrast with *soft hyphen.*

hard space In word processing programs, a space specially formatted so that the program does not introduce a line break at the space's location. Hard spaces often are used to keep two words together, such as San Diego or light pen.

hardware The physical components of a computer system. Contrast with *software.*

Harvard Graphics A business graphics program for IBM-compatible microcomputer systems from Software Publishing Corporation. It is a versatile and easy-to-use program for producing business related presentation graphics. The program requires little knowledge of graphics presentation principles because it guides the user through each step of the process and produces output that meets high standards of aesthetics and professional graphics.

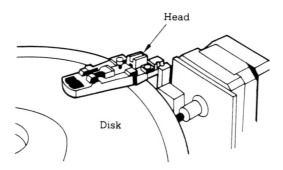

head

head   The part of the disk drive that actually reads information from the disk surface, or writes information to it.

head crash   Collision of the read/write head with the recording surface of a hard disk, resulting in loss of data. Usually caused by contamination of the disk, such as from a tiny particle of smoke or dust or from a fingerprint.

header   (1) First part of a message, containing all the necessary information for directing the message to its destination(s). (2) Top margin of a page, usually the title of the book, the name of the chapter, the page number, and so on.

help   (1) Handy function available on many systems. Supplies the user with additional information on how the system or program works. (2) On screen reference material providing assistance with the program.

help balloon   An operating system and application program user help aid that tags a desired object on screen with a comic book style "balloon" full of information on how to use that object.

Trash
To discard an item or eject a disk, drag it to the Trash. To permanently remove all items in the Trash, choose Empty Trash from the Special Menu.

help balloon   Trash

hertz   Cycles per second. Abbreviated Hz.

heuristic method   A method of solving problems that consists of a sequence of trials yielding approximate results, with control of the progression toward an acceptable final result.

Hewlett-Packard Company (HP) A major manufacturer of computer equipment; founded in 1939 by William Hewlett and David Packard in a garage behind Packard's California home. HP has introduced several calculators, computer series, workstations, laser printers, and many other electronic products.

hidden character A character that is not normally printed or displayed for example, in a word processor, an embedded control character.

hidden file Hidden files occupy disk space but do not appear in directory listings. Files are hidden to prevent their display or change. Sometimes called invisible files. You cannot display, erase, or copy hidden files.

hidden line (1) When displaying a three-dimensional object, any line that would normally be obscured from the viewer's sight by the mass of the object itself, visible as a result of the projection. (2) Lines that have been drawn on the screen in background color and will not become visible until the colors are switched. (3) Lines of a diagram that are invisible.

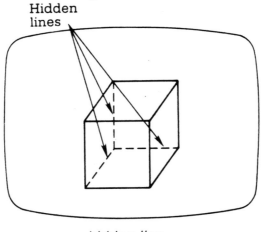

hidden line

hierarchical file system (HFS) A pyramid-like file system where each object is linked to those beneath it.

hierarchy The order in which arithmetic operations, within a formula, or computer program instruction will be executed by the computer.

high-density disk A floppy disk that holds more information than a double-density disk.

high-level programming language Any programming language that allows users to write instructions in a familiar notation rather than in a machine code. Each statement in a high-level language corresponds to several machine-code instructions. Contrast with *low-level language.*

highlighting (1) Process of making a display segment stand out by causing blinking, brightening, underlining, by reversing the background and the character images, such as dark characters on a light background, or creating a color combination that draws attention to it. (2) Highlighting is often used in word processing and page design programs as a means of selecting characters that are to be deleted, copied, or otherwise acted upon.

HIGH-RESOLUTION

LOW-RESOLUTION

high-resolution

high-resolution (1) Pertaining to the quality and accuracy of detail that can be represented by a graphics display. Resolution quality depends upon the number of basic image-forming units (pixels) within a picture image — the greater the number, the higher the resolution. High-resolution pictures, produced by a large number of pixels, are sharper than low-resolution pictures. (2) In printing, resolution is defined as the number of dots per inch (dpi) that are printed. In general, laser printing is usually 300 or 600 dpi, typesetters and imagesetters can produce output at 1000 dpi, 2000 dpi, or more.

Hoff, Ted In 1971, as an engineer with Intel Corporation, Hoff led the team that designed the 4004 microprocessor. The single chip contained 2250 transistors, and all of the components of a full-sized central processing unit. This microchip caused the computer industry and its suppliers to rethink the future role of the computer. The first advertisement for the 4004 appeared in an issue of *Electronic News* in November, 1971. By 1974, Intel sold more microprocessors than the entire population of mainframes and minicomputers. See *Intel Corporation.*

Ted Hoff

Hollerith, Herman (1860-1929) As a statistician and employee of the Census Bureau, he proposed using punched cards in conjunction with electromechanical relays to accomplish simple additions and sortings needed in the 1890 census. It was this invention of Hollerith's that launched the information handling revolution. Afterward, many others followed who also made significant contributions leading to the development of the computer in the 1940's. Hollerith was recognized as the father of the first data processing devices. The company Hollerith set up to manufacture his punched card tabulator became one of the parents of the IBM Corporation.

Herman Hollerith

Hollerith Tabulating Machine The first statistical machine that operated on the punched card principle. The functions of the Hollerith Tabulating Machine were to record, compile, and tabulate census data. The machine was completed in time for the 1890 census for which it was first employed. The census data were punched into cards which were then manually fed into an electromagnetic counter and a sorting box. This electric tabulating system permitted the completion of the 1890 census in two and one-half years, one third the time required in the census ten years earlier.

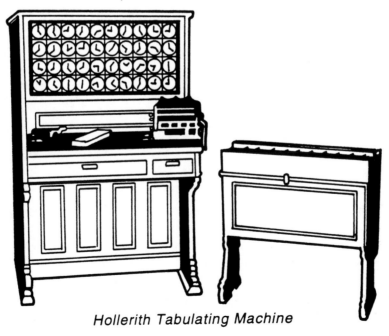

Hollerith Tabulating Machine

home computer

home computer A personal computer designed and priced for use in the home.

home key Keyboard function that directs the cursor to its home position, usually in the top left portion of the display screen.

Hopper, Grace Murray (1906-1992) Mathematician and programmer who developed programs for the ASCC and early UNIVAC computers. Later became a pioneer in the field of computer languages, writing the first practical compiler program and playing an important role in the development of COBOL. She was affectionately known as Grandma COBOL, The Grand Lady of Software, and Amazing Grace. Computer pioneer Rear Admiral Grace Hopper published many papers and articles on software and programming languages, and was a frequent speaker on University campuses. Grace Hopper was an inspiration to computer programmers and made many contributions to the world of information technology.

Grace Hopper

horizon software Software for many uses such as word processors, spreadsheets, and database management programs.

host The central or controlling computer in a computer network.

housekeeping Computer operations that do not directly contribute toward the desired results, but are a necessary part of a program, such as initialization, set-up, and clean-up operations. Sometimes called bookkeeping.

hub A device that physically connects two or more cables together. The hub is the central point in the star network topology.

hung system A computer that has experienced a system failure sufficiently grave to prevent further processing.

HyperCard An implementation of a hypertext system for the Apple Macintosh family of computers. A HyperCard document consists of a series of cards collected together in a stack; each card can contain text, graphics and sound. Items on the cards can be linked together in a variety of different ways.

hypermedia A term describing hypertext-based systems that combine text, graphics, sound, and video with traditional data. In a hypertext system, you select a word or phrase and give a command to see related text. In a hypermedia system, such a command reveals related graphics image, sounds, and even snippets of animation or video. HyperCard is an example of a hypermedia application.

HyperTalk The programming language used in the HyperCard program to manipulate HyperCard stacks. HyperTalk implements object-oriented programming principles.

hypertext An assembly of images, sound and text connected by electronic links, which facilitates nonlinear reading and writing.

hyphenation In page layout and word processing programs, an automatic operation that hyphenates words on certain lines to improve word spacing.

Hz An abbreviation for *Hertz*, which is a measure of frequency; number of cycles per second. Microprocessor clock speeds are measured in Hertz. The more Hertz, the faster the clock. Named after Heinrich R. Hertz.

I-beam pointer In a graphical user interface, a special pointer shaped like a capital "I" that indicates the insertion point for text editing.

IBM Corporation The International Business Machines Corporation is the world's largest computer company. It started in New York City in 1911 when the Computing-Tabulating-Recording (CTR) Company was formed by a merger of four companies. Thomas J. Watson, Sr. became the general manager in 1914. Over the next decade, Watson turned CTR into an international enterprise. In 1924 the company was renamed IBM. IBM started making computers in 1953 and has since introduced computers of all sizes. A few models produced by IBM include the 650, 701, 702, 703, 704, 705, 709, 1401, 1410, 1620, 1790, and 1794 mainframe computers. In April started making computers in 1953 and has since introduced computers of all sizes. A few models produced by IBM include the 650, 701, 702, 703, 704, 705, 709, 1401, 1410, 1620, 1790, and 1794 main frame computers. In April 1964, IBM introduced the third generation of computers with the introduction of the System/360 family of computers. Throughout the 1970s, IBM introduced several minicomputer systems: System/3, System/34, System/36, System/38, Series 1, 8100, and AS/400. In 1981, IBM introduced the IBM Personal Computer. In 1987, IBM introduced the PS/2 series of personal computers. Today, product lines of the IBM Corporation span personal computers to large mainframes. See *Watson, Thomas J., Jr.* and *Watson, Thomas J., Sr.*

IBM PC compatible A term for personal computers that adhere closely to the functionality of personal computers in the IBM PC family. PC compatibles, as opposed to "clones," have never necessarily had to look like standard IBM PC designs, and some manufacturers have insisted on incorporating proprietary, non-standard features in their "compatibles" even while maintaining general compatibility with the MS-DOS, Intel-based features of the IBM PC family.

IBM Personal Computer

IBM Personal Computer (IBM PC)   August 12, 1981, came and went, but nothing would ever be the same again. That day, the IBM Corporation introduced a Personal Computer based on the Intel 8088 microprocessor. The machine went on to become the most significant technology to hit the world since the telephone. Although the IBM PC was not the first, it legitimized the machines in the computer market. It has transformed the way millions of people work, spawned new industries and made computer technology less mysterious. The PC created the home computer movement, allowing people to work out of their living room and "commute" by sending reports to the office over the phone. IBM set the stage for clones when it announced the PC by deciding not to block other companies from providing software or accessories for its PC. It reasoned that if the technology was "open," or non-proprietary, the market for the machines would grow faster. But that decision soon led to the creation of clones of the entire computer. Today, every nation from Hong Kong to Hungary has a local industry cranking out inexpensive PC clones. There are three machines in the PC line: IBM PC, IBM PC-XT and IBM PC-AT.

IBM Personal System/1 (PS/1)   A home computer from IBM Corporation introduced in 1990. The PS/1 computer uses an Intel 80286 microprocessor and comes in a small, attractive case, with a color VGA display and a modem built in. The computer contains about everything an ordinary computer user is likely to need.

IBM Personal System/2 (PS/2)   A series of personal computers from IBM Corporation introduced in 1987. These computers were designed to replace the IBM Personal Computer line: IBM PC, IBM PC-XT, IBM PC-AT. The PS/2 machines are based on the Intel 8086, 80286, 80386, and 80486 microprocessors. The IBM PS/2 runs all or almost all the software developed for the IBM Personal Computer.

111

IBM RS/6000 An IBM family of RISC-based workstations introduced in 1990.

IC An acronym for Integrated Circuit, an electronic circuit etched on a tiny germanium or silicon chip. IC's are categorized by the number of elements they hold.

icon A tiny on-screen pictorial representation of a software function. A symbol used on the display screen to represent some feature of the program. For example, in one program, an icon representing a waste-paper basket is selected if you want to erase information. Many workstations in a networking environment, for instance, use a mailbox icon to symbolize an electronic mail-reading utility.

 QuarkXPress® DesignStudio

icon

IDE A hardware technology for connecting disk drives to computers.

idle time Time that a computer system is available for use but is not in actual operation.

IEEE See *Institute of Electrical and Electronic Engineers.*

IEEE Computer Society A section of the Institute of Electrical and Electronics Engineers. Publishes a monthly periodical on computer graphics and applications.

IFIP Acronym for International Federation of Information Processing, a multinational affiliation of professional groups concerned with information processing. The U.S. representative from 1960-90 was AFIPS. Today the U.S. representative is FOCUS.

illegal character Character or combination of bits not accepted by the computer as a valid or known representation.

illustration program A program for creating and manipulating object-oriented graphics, as opposed to creating and manipulating pixel images. See *draw program* and *paint program.*

Illustrator See *Adobe Illustrator.*

image (1) Exact logical duplicate stored in a different medium. If the computer user displays the contents of memory on a display screen, he or she will see an image of memory. (2) In computer graphics, the output form of graphics data, such as a drawn representation of a graphics file. (3) A visual representation of an object, figure, or event in any visual art.

image

image analysis The process of extracting useful information from images, such as estimating types of surface ground cover from satellite photographs.

image compression As applied to graphics computer systems and scanners, encoding the data describing an image in a more compact form to reduce storage requirements or transmission time.

image enhancement The process of improving the appearance of all or part of a graphics image through such techniques as coloring, shading, highlighting, edge enhancement, gray-scale manipulation, zooming, reverse video, blinking, smoothing, or sharpening.

image processing Method for processing pictorial information by a computer system. Involves inputting graphics information into a computer system, storing it, working with it, and outputting it to an output device.

imagesetter A typesetting device that can transfer output of a desktop publishing system directly to paper or film. Imagesetters commonly print at high resolution (from 1200 dpi to over 3000 dpi). Imagesetters are professional typesetting machines that use chemical photo-reproduction techniques to produce high resolution output.

impact printer Data printout device that imprints by momentary pressure of raised type against paper, using ink or ribbon as a color medium. Contrast with *nonimpact printer*.

import To bring information from one system or program into another. PageMaker, for example, can import EPS files created by Adobe Illustrator, MacPaint files created by SuperPaint or text files created by Microsoft Word.

index hole Hole punched through a floppy disk that can be read by the electro-optical system in the disk drive to locate accurately the beginning of sector zero on the disk.

industry standard architecture (ISA) The original design the IBM Corporation used for manufacturing their personal computers. ISA is the de facto standard for personal computers.

industrial robot Reprogrammable, multifunctional manipulator designed to move material parts, tools, or specialized devices through variable programmed motions for the performance of a variety of tasks. Unlike other forms of automation, robots can be programmed to do a variety of tasks, making them the most versatile of manufacturing tools.

industrial robot

infection The presence within a computer system of a virus or Trojan Horse.

information Meaningful and useful facts that are extracted from data fed to a computer. Processed data; data that is organized, meaningful, and useful.

information retrieval The process used to recover specific information from computer storage.

information superhighway Every future scenario for our information society projects a world linked entirely by telecommunications, a world in which people interact daily with vast amounts of data — text, sound, and video images — that circle the globe at the speed of light. These data will be delivered through now-merging computer, telephone and cable television technologies. To some extent, this future scenario is already a reality. Today people throughout the world are using a giant worldwide telecommunications network called the Internet. The Internet is a network of networks; a multitude of computers all around the world, communicating via phone lines and any other media that can support the Internet's special communication language. The Internet, with its masses of data, millions of users, and endless opportunities for the exchange of ideas, is a main road system for the phenomenon now being called the information superhighway. The expansion of the Internet and advances in telecommunications equipment are sure to increase the power and extent of this highway.

initialization Process of formatting a diskette so that it is ready for use. Initialization erases any previous information that happens to be on the diskette.

ink jet printer A printer that sprays ink from jet nozzles onto the paper. A nozzle emits a continuous stream of ink droplets that are selectively guided either to the paper or to a gutter where they may be recycled for re-use or sent into a discard container. Ink jet printers produce high-quality printouts.

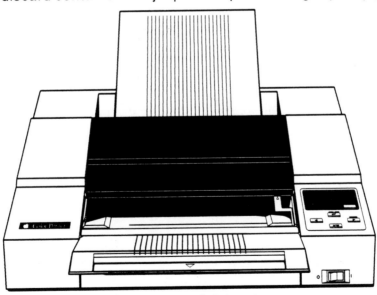

ink jet printer

input Introduction of data from an external storage medium into a computer's internal storage unit. Contrast with *output*.

input device A hardware device that enables the user to communicate with a computer system. Examples of input devices are keyboard, mouse, light pen, track ball, or graphics tablet. Contrast with *output device*.

input/output device Unit used to get data from the human user into the central processing unit, and to transfer data from the computer's internal storage to some storage or output device. See *input device, output device,* and *peripheral equipment.*

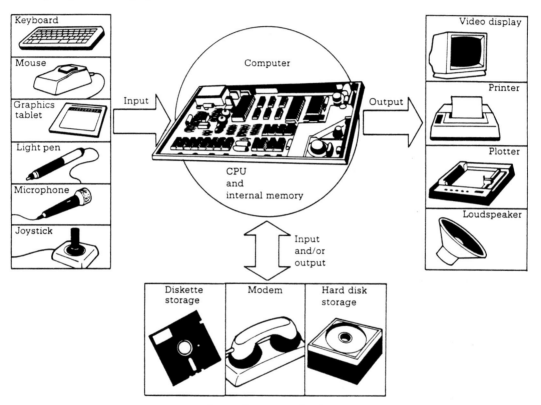

input/output device

insert To create and place entities, figures, text, or information on a CRT or into an emerging design on the display.

insertion point Position at which text is entered into a document.

installation General term for a particular computer system.

installation program A program that prepares a software program to run in the computer. It customizes elements of the new program so a specific computer system can use it.

Institute of Electrical and Electronic Engineers (IEEE) A professional engineering organization founded in 1963 for the furthering of education, research, and standards in the electronics and electrical fields. IEEE has a strong interest in computer technology. It sponsors many educational opportunities and publications for members.

instruction Defines an operation to be performed by the computer. "ADD A TO B" is an instruction.

instruction set A set of simple operation commands that a computer is capable of performing.

integer A number which may be positive, negative or zero. It does not have a fractional part. Examples of integers are 47, 82, and -156.

integrated circuit (IC) An electronic circuit etched on a tiny germanium or silicon chip. Integrated circuits are categorized by the number of elements (transistors, resistors, etc.) they hold. See *large-scale integration (LSI), medium-scale integration (MSI), small-scale integration (SSI), ultra large-scale integration (ULSI)*, and *very large-scale integration (VLSI)*.

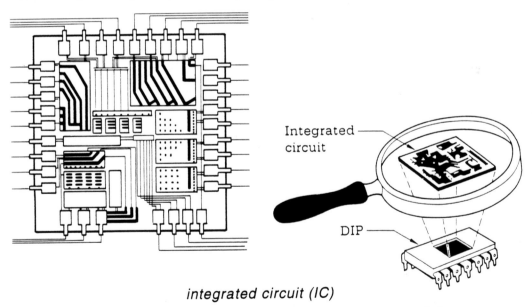

integrated circuit (IC)

integrated software An applications software package containing programs to perform more than one function. The package typically includes related word processing, spreadsheet, database, and graphics programs. Since the information from the electronic spreadsheet may be shared with the database manager and the word processor (and vice versa), this software is called integrated.

integration The integration of electronic components grew out of many different technologies, and its origins are thus hard to trace. The problem was to produce increasingly complex and small integrated circuits. In the case of a computer, the time taken by a signal to go from one circuit to the next limits its performance. In the early 1970s, engineers developed LSI (Large Scale Integration), whereby a single chip could hold around 500 components. By the late 1970s, LSI had been upgraded to VLSI (Very Large Scale Integration), which allowed up to 10,000 active elements. The level of integration of components on single chips has continued to advance at an exponential rate. Today a single chip is capable of containing millions of active elements.

integrity (1) Preservation of programs or data for their intended purpose. (2) Adherence to a code of behavior or ethics. (3) The integrity of data concerns its accuracy, completeness, and safety.

Intel Corporation A leading manufacturer of semiconductor devices that was founded in 1968 by Robert Noyce and Gordon Moore in Mountain View, California. In 1971, Intel engineer Marcian E. "Ted' Hoff, designed the 4-bit 4004 microprocessor chip. Throughout the years Intel has developed a wide variety of chips and board-level products. In 1994, Intel, the world's largest producer of semiconductor chips, and Hewlett-Packard, a large computer maker, agreed to work together to develop a single chip to run in both personal computers and larger workstations. The chip should emerge by the year 2000. Some Intel chips and their processing speeds are listed below:

Chip	Introduced in	MIPS
8088	1979	0.33
80286	1982	1.2
80386	1985	5.5
80486	1989	20.0
Pentium	1993	112.0
Pentium Pro	1995	250.0
P7	1997	Unknown

The name Intel is a contraction of Integrated Electronics.

Intel 8080 An 8-bit microprocessor introduced in 1974 by Intel Corporation.

Intel 8086 A 16-bit microprocessor introduced in 1978 by Intel Corporation.

Intel 8088 A 16-bit microprocessor introduced in 1978 by Intel Corporation. This microprocessor was used in the original IBM Personal Computer.

Intel 80286 A microprocessor introduced in 1984 by Intel Corporation. This microprocessor was used in the IBM Personal Computer AT.

Intel 80386 DX A microprocessor introduced in 1986 by Intel Corporation.

Intel 80386 SX A microprocessor introduced in 1988 by Intel Corporation.

Intel 80486 DX A microprocessor introduced in 1989 by Intel Corporation.

Intel 80486 SX A microprocessor introduced in 1990 by Intel Corporation.

Intel 88000 A family of 32-bit RISC microprocessors introduced in 1988 by Intel Corporation.

interactive program Computer program that permits data to be entered or the flow of the program to be modified during its execution.

interface A hardware and/or software link which enables two systems, or a computer and its peripherals, to operate as a single, integrated system. A shared boundary.

interface card The hardware board containing a device port that is placed inside the computer's system unit which lets you attach a device to the computer.

internal hard disk A hard disk designed to fit within a computer's case and to use the computer's power supply.

internal storage Addressable storage directly controlled by the central processing unit. Used to store programs while they are being executed and data while they are being processed. Also called immediate access storage, internal memory, main storage, and primary storage. Contrast with *auxiliary storage*.

Internet The largest network of computers in the world. The Internet provides E-mail, file transfer, news, remote login, and access to thousands of databases. You can play games, engage in conversations with people around the world, and build your own library of journals, books and images.

interpreter Language translator that converts each source-language statement into machine code and executes it immediately, statement by statement. Program that performs interpretation. Contrast with *compiler*.

interrupt Signal that, when activated, causes the hardware to transfer program control to some specific location in internal storage, thus breaking the normal flow of the program being executed. After the interrupt has been processed, program control is again returned to the interrupted program.

inverse video See *reverse video*.

invert

invert (1) To turn over; reverse. To highlight text or objects by reversing the on-screen display or printout. For example, to invert the colors on a monochrome display means to change light to dark and dark to light. (2) To convert a logic value to its opposite, i.e., zero to one and one to zero.

I/O system See *input/output system*.

ISA See *industry standard architecture*.

iterative (1) A technique for solving a problem by repeatedly applying the same operations. (2) In fractal geometry, the repeated evaluation of successive output points.

jacket The plastic cover for a disk. It has holes and slots cut into it to expose the hub and afford the head-of-disk drive access to the disk. 5.25-inch disks use a stiff plastic jacket, with glued or crimped seams. 3.5-inch disks use rigid plastic envelopes, with spring-loaded sliding metal shutters to protect the disk surface from being touched accidentally.

Jacquard, Joseph Marie (1752-1834) Built a weaving machine (Jacquard loom) that used a line of punched cards to control automatically the patterns woven. Some people feel that Jacquard's machine was the beginning of factory automation. Jacquard did not invent the punch card controlled loom. But he improved upon previous versions so much that his was the first automated loom to achieve widespread commercial success. In 1812 there were 11,000 Jacquard looms in France alone. The loom inspired both Charles Babbage (1792-1871) and Herman Hollerith (1860-1929) and, through them, the data processing and computer industries.

Joseph Jacquard

jaggies In a computer graphics display, the stairstepped or saw-toothed effect of diagonals, circles, and curves.

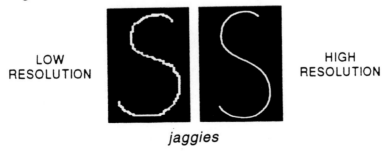

LOW RESOLUTION   HIGH RESOLUTION

jaggies

121

jargon The vocabulary peculiar to a group or profession. Computer jargon includes the terms in this dictionary.

job Collection of specified tasks constituting a unit of work for a computer, such as a program or related group of programs used as a unit.

job control language (JCL) On mainframe systems, a control language that enables programmers to specify batch processing operations, which the computer then carries out. The language defines a job and the resources it requires from the computer system, including constraints on the job, such as time limits. The language is more often interpreted than compiled.

job queue Set of programs and data currently making its way through the computer. In most operating systems, each job is brought into the queue and is processed (given control of the computer) when it is the "oldest" job within its own priority. An exception to this is a job of higher priority that has not yet obtained sufficient resources to be processed.

Jobs, Steven (born 1955) Co-founder (with Stephen Wozniak) of Apple Computer, Inc., developer of several microcomputer systems. In 1977, Jobs and Wozniak introduced the Apple II microcomputer. This popular computer became known as the Volkswagon of computers. In 1984, Apple Computer announced the Macintosh computer. This was Steve Job's electronic baby. He shaped it, nourished it, and pampered it into life. The Macintosh has become one of the most exciting and easy-to-use computers of all time. In 1985, after a management disagreement with Apple president John Sculley, Jobs left Apple Computer and established a new firm, called NeXT, Inc. In 1988, Jobs unveiled the NeXT computer system. See *Apple Computer, Inc.* and *Wozniak, Stephen.*

Steven Jobs

joystick A lever, pivoted to move in any direction that controls the movement of a cursor on a display screen. Similar to a mouse, but used mostly when playing video games.

justification The insertion of extra space between words in lines so that both the left and right margins are even and smooth.

Kb An abbreviation for *Kilobyte*. One Kb is 1024 bytes.

Kahn, Philippe A former student of Niklaus Wirth, developed a Turbo Pascal compiler for microcomputers. Turbo Pascal is the most popular version of the Pascal language for microcomputers. Kahn's company, Borland International, Inc., went on to develop several software systems for microcomputers. Kahn left Borland in 1995 to start a new software company called Starfish Software. Products of the new company are Sidekick, a personal information manager and Dashboard, a Windows utility.

Philippe Kahn

Kemeny, John George (1926-1992) In 1964, with Thomas Kurtz, at Dartmouth College, designed the computer language BASIC, an easy-to-learn, easy-to-use algebraic programming language. BASIC, which eased the process of debugging and changing programs, soon became the bible for beginners in computing. In the early 1950s, Kemeny joined the Dartmouth University faculty. There, he held various positions, including that of college president from 1970 to 1981. In 1983, Kemeny and Kurtz developed True BASIC, a more powerful version of their legendary language. See *BASIC* and *Kurtz, Thomas*.

John Kemeny

Kermit A file transfer protocol used for more error-free modem communications.

kernel Set of programs in an operating system that implement the most primitive of that system's functions. The core of an operating system and stays resident in internal memory at all times. See *shell*.

kerning Adjusting the space between characters to create wider or tighter spacing. Reduction of excess white space between specific letter pairs. For example, the pair To can be placed more closely together than the pair Tk because the arm of the T fits over the top of the o. Kerning is especially important with large type sizes.

key (1) Control field or fields that identify a record. (2) Field that determines the position of a record in a sorted sequence. (3) Lever on a manually operated machine, such as a typewriter or visual display keyboard. (4) To enter data into a system by means of a keyboard.

keyboard Input device used to key programs and data into the computer's storage. Since the keyboard is the most frequently used part of the computer, a good keyboard is an essential part of any computer system intended for business purposes.

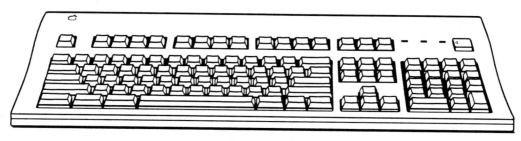

keyboard

keyboard template A plastic or cardboard card with adhesive that can be pressed onto the keyboard to explain the way a program configures the keyboard.

keystroke Action of pressing a single key or a combination of keys on a keyboard. Speed in many data entry jobs is measured in keystrokes per minute.

keyword (1) One of the significant and informative words in a title or document that describe the content of that document. (2) Primary element in a programming language statement, such as LET, PRINT, and INPUT in the BASIC programming language. A keyword is followed by a series of arguments used by the keyword to complete a task. (3) Set of words that have special meaning to a computer program. For example, DIR is a command that directs the operating system to produce a DIRECTORY of a disk.

Kilby, Jack St. Clair (born 1923)   Kilby was the first to conceive of integrating transistors, resistors, and capacitors on a single chip of germanium while at Texas Instruments in 1958, but he didn't get around to developing a chip on which the devices could be interconnected, except by hand. In 1961, the U.S. Patent Office ended up granting the patent to Robert Noyce of Fairchild Semiconductor, whose description for interconnection was ruled to be adequate. Both Kilby and Noyce are credited as co-inventors of the integrated circuit. In 1981, Kilby was inducted into the National Inventors Hall of Fame. See *Noyce, Robert.*

Jack Kilby

Kildall, Gary (1942-1994)   In 1977, he developed CP/M, an operating system for microcomputers. CP/M became a standard operating system for microcomputers before the IBM PC (and PC-DOS) was introduced in 1981. CP/M became a popular program for two reasons; it eliminated the need for manufacturers to design individual operating systems, and CP/M was the first operating system designed to control floppy disk drives. Kildall later developed DR LOGO, his own version of the popular LOGO programming language.

Gary Kildall

kill (1) To terminate a process before it reaches its natural conclusion. (2) Method of erasing information. (3) To stop, frequently to abort.

kilobyte Specifically, 1024 bytes. Commonly thought of as 1000. Abbreviated K and used as a suffix when describing memory size. Thus, 24K really means a 24 x 1024 = 24,576-byte memory system. Sometimes abbreviated Kb.

knowbots Programs that search through networks locating specific information; robotic librarians.

knowledge base Database of knowledge about a particular subject. Contains facts, data, beliefs, assumptions, and procedures needed for problem solution.

knowledge domain In artificial intelligence, an area of problem solving expertise.

knowledge engineering Engineering discipline whereby knowledge is integrated into computer systems to solve complex problems normally requiring a high level of human expertise.

Kurtz, Thomas E. (born 1928) In 1964, with John Kemeny, at Dartmouth College, designed the computer language BASIC, an easy-to-learn, easy-to-use algebraic programming language. Their goal was to develop a simple and powerful programming language that students of all disciplines could learn easily. Kurtz and Kemeny tried to impress upon members of the educational community the philosophy that an understanding of computers is as necessary to life as being able to read and write. Furthermore, the two believe that computers should be as accessible as a library. This philosophy is now being implemented in schools across the United States. In 1983, Kurtz and Kemeny developed True BASIC, a more powerful version of their original BASIC. See *BASIC* and *Kemeny, John.*

Thomas Kurtz

label Identifier or name used in a computer program to identify or describe an instruction, statement, message, data value, record, item, or file.

LAN See *local area network*.

landscape orientation An orientation in which the data has a width greater than its height. Contrast with *portrait orientation*. See *orientation*.

landscape orientation

language Set of rules, representations, and conventions used to convey information. A way of passing instructions to the computer other than through direct input of number codes. Programming languages are characterized as low-level or high-level.

language translator A program that transforms statements from one language to another without changing their meaning. A compiler is a language translator.

laptop computer

laptop computer A personal computer, small and portable enough to be used comfortably in the lap of a person seated in an automobile or an airplane. Laptop computers are battery powered in their normal operation. Laptop computers today feature full-sized keyboards, flat-screen monitors that fold up and down, hard disks, floppy disks, and powerful microprocessors.

large-scale integration (LSI) Process of placing between 3,000-100,000 electronic components on a single chip. See *integrated circuit*.

128

laser Acronym for Light Amplification by Simulated Emission of Radiation, the technology that uses the principle of amplification of electromagnetic waves by simulated emission of radiation and operates in the infrared, visible, or ultraviolet region. A device emitting coherent photon or electromagnetic energy.

LaserJet A series of desktop laser printers from Hewlett-Packard Company. Introduced in 1984, it set the standard for the desktop laser printer market.

laser printer A printer that uses a light beam to transfer images to paper. Laser printers print a full page at a time. A laser is used to "paint" the dots of light onto a photographic drum or belt and then transferred onto the paper. In 1975, the IBM Corporation introduced the first laser printer, called the IBM 3800, which was designed for high-speed printing. In 1978, the Xerox Corporation introduced the Xerox 9700 high-speed printer. In 1984, the Hewlett-Packard Company introduced the first desktop laser printer, which has revolutionized personal computer printing and has spawned desktop publishing. Desktop laser printers is technically more like an office copier than a conventional printer. They are very fast in operation and relatively silent.

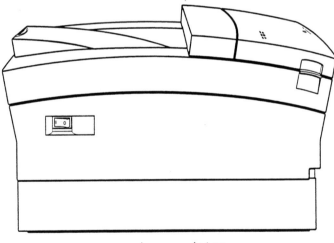

laser printer

LaserWriter A series of desktop laser printers from Apple Computer, Inc.

launch To start a program.

layer (1) In computer graphics drawing programs, an overlay on which text or images can be stored. In SuperPaint, for example, you can create illustrations on two layers: a paint layer for bit-mapped graphics and a draw layer for object-oriented graphics. In some graphics programs you can draw and paint on many different layers. (2) Third dimension in a 3-D array.

129

layering (1) Logical concept that associates subgroups of graphic data within a single drawing. Allows a user to view only those parts of a drawing being worked on and reduces the confusion that might result from viewing all parts of a very complex file. (2) Organizing data in layers.

layout (1) In desktop publishing, the design or process of arranging text and graphics on a page. (2) The arrangement of data items on a data record. (3) Overall design or plan, such as system flowcharts, schematics, diagrams, format for printer output, and makeup of a document (book).

LCD An acronym for Liquid Crystal Display, the monitor type used by many laptop and portable computers.

LCD printer Short for Liquid Crystal Display printer, an electrophotographic printer that uses an electrostatically charged drum to transfer toner to a piece of paper. Similar to laser printers and LED printers.

leader (1) In page layout and word processing programs, a row of dots and dashes that provide a path for the eye to follow across the page. Leaders are sometimes used in table of contents to lead the reader's eye from the entry to the page number. (2) Blank section of tape at the beginning of a reel of magnetic tape.

leading The vertical spacing between lines of type, measured from baseline to baseline. Font styles which have long ascenders and descenders need more leading than fonts that don't. In publishing, the font size and leading is described as a fraction. For example, 10/12 (which is read "10 on 12") indicates 10 point type with 2 point leading.

leading edge (1) In optical scanning, the edge of the document or page that enters the read position first. (2) Buzz word implying technological leadership: "on the leading edge of technology."

leading zeros Zeros placed to the left of a number without changing the value of a number.

leased line A communications circuit or telephone line reserved for the permanent use of a specific customer.

LED printer Short for Light Emitting Diode printer, an electrophotographic printer that uses an electrostatically charged drum to transfer toner to a piece of paper. Similar to laser printers and LCS printers.

left justification A method of aligning text so that each line of text is flush against the left margin, leaving a ragged or uneven right margin.

legend (1) Text beneath a graph; it explains the colors, shading, or symbols used to label the data points. (2) Text that describes or explains a graphic.

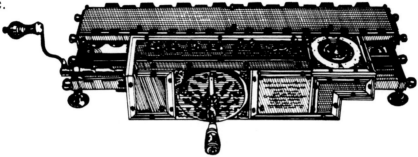

Leibniz's calculator

Leibniz's calculator Calculating machine designed by Gottfried von Leibniz. Performed addition and subtraction in the same manner as Pascal's calculator; however, additional gears were included in the machine that enabled it to multiply directly.

Leibniz, Gottfried Wilhelm (1646-1716) German mathematician who in 1672 invented a calculating machine superior to Pascal's calculator, in 1673 introduced a system of the calculus, and in 1693 he recognized the energy of motion and of position. Leibniz's calculating machine could perform addition, subtraction, multiplication and division. Leibniz went on to make a killing in the marketplace. Not that he was just in it for the money: "For it is unworthy of excellent men to lose hours like slaves in the labor of calculation," he wrote, "which could safely be relegated to anyone else if machines were used."

Gottfried Leibniz

letter quality printing High-quality output produced by some printers. Laser printers, daisy-wheel printers and ink-jet printers are letter quality printers. High-end, 24-pin dot matrix printers provide near letter quality printing.

library (1) Published collection of programs, routines, and subroutines available to every user of the computer. (2) A storage area, usually on hard disk or a diskette, used to store programs. (3) A collection of items, such as clip art, intended for inclusion in other programs.

license agreement   A written agreement provided by a software developer that defines the user's rights to the software. Use of the software implies the user's acceptance of the agreement's terms.

light pen   Electronic input device that resembles a pen and can be used to write or sketch on the screen of a graphics display. The user points the light pen at a location on the graphics display. When the electron gun illuminates the phosphor, the light pen detects the light and sends a signal to the graphics system, which records the pixel event at that moment.

light pen

line art   Artwork containing only blacks and whites with no shading. Line art can be reproduced accurately by low to medium resolution printers.

line feed (LF)   Operation that advances printer paper by one line.

line graph   Graph made by connecting data points with a line. Shows the variations of data over time or the relationships between two numeric variables.

line printer   A printer that assembles all characters on a line at one time and prints them out practically simultaneously. Line printers are high-speed printing devices that are usually connected to mainframes and minicomputers.

line spacing   The space between lines of text. See *leading*.

link (1) In data communications, a physical connection between one location and another whose function is to transmit data, including satellite links. (2) In hypertext systems, connections between one document and another.

linkage editor (1) A system program that binds together related object module program segments so they may be run as a unit. (2) Part of the operating system that links the object code with any necessary library routines.

liquid crystal display (LCD) A flat display used in many portable computers because it is small, and requires little power. The display is made of two sheets of polarizing material sandwiched together with a liquid crystal solution between them. Images are produced when electric currents cause the liquid crystals to align so light cannot shine through.

Lisa A microcomputer introduced in the early 1980s by Apple Computer, Inc. It featured a graphical user interface and a mouse. The Lisa had its own Apple-generated operating system, called the Lisa Operating System. This was designed to perform file management, memory management, event handling and exception handling. The Lisa was built around the Motorola 68000 microprocessor. The Lisa was the forerunner of the Apple Macintosh microcomputer.

```
(DEFINE COUNT2 (LAMBDA (L)
    (PROG (N)
        (SETQ N 0)
    LOOP
        (COND ((NULL L) RETURN
    N)))
        (SETQ N (ADD1 N))
        (SETQ L (CDR L))
        (GO LOOP)) ))
```

LISP program

LISP Acronym for LISt Processing, high-level programming language primarily designed to process data consisting of lists. Especially suited for text manipulation and analysis.

list A data structure in which each item of information has attached to it one or more links or pointers which refer to other items.

load (1) To read information into the storage of a computer. See *get*. (2) To put a diskette into a disk drive. (3) To insert paper into a printer.

local area network (LAN) A privately run communications network of several machines located within a mile or so of one another.

local variable A variable that has meaning only within a particular function, subroutine or program.

logarithmic graph In presentation graphics, a graph displayed with a y-axis incremented exponentially in powers of 10. On an ordinary y-axis, the 10 is followed by 20, 30, 40, 50, and so on. On a logarithmic scale, however, 10 is followed by 100, 1000, 10,000, 100,000, and so on.

logic bomb A program or a section of code built into a program that lies dormant until a predefined condition is met. When that condition occurs, the bomb goes off with a result that is neither expected nor desired. Time bombs explode frequently. Depending on who authored the bomb and how many generations of backups it contaminated, the recovery effort ranges from mildly inconvenient to nearly impossible. See *virus*.

logical operations Computer operations that are logical in nature, such as logical decisions. Contrast with arithmetic operations and data transfer operations, which involve no decision.

login The process of notifying a network that you are using a specific workstation. Login defines the start of a session.

LOGO High-level programming language that assumes the user has access to some type of graphics terminal. Designed for students and easily employed by those in the younger age groups, it has wide-ranging application in graphic reports of business and industry. Highly interactive, permitting users to learn quickly how to draw geometric patterns and pictures on the screen. One important feature of LOGO is turtle graphics. Turtle graphics enable the programmer to make simple drawings by telling the "turtle" on the screen to move forward, right, left, and so on. Once he or she masters the simple drawing environment, the programmer starts to discover the more sophisticated features of the language. Developed in 1968 at the Massachusetts Institute of Technology by Seymour Papert. See *turtle graphics*.

log off To terminate connection with the computer.

log on Action by which a user begins a terminal session.

logout The process of notifying a network that you are ending a session on a specific workstation. Logout defines the end of a session.

loop Sequence of instructions in a program that can be executed repetitively until certain specified conditions are satisfied.

Lotus Development Corporation A software company founded by Mitchell D. Kapor in 1981. The company is best known for its flagship product, Lotus 1-2-3, a popular spreadsheet program; however, it has also produced other business application programs such as Symphony, an integrated program, and Agenda, an information management program.

Lotus 1-2-3 A spreadsheet developed by Lotus Development Corporation. Introduced in 1982, it was the first integrated program developed for the IBM Personal Computer. Lotus 1-2-3 was the first program to include graphics, database management along with spreadsheet capabilities.

low end Computer jargon for an inexpensive product, from the bottom of a company's product list.

low-level language Machine-dependent programming language translated by an assembler into instructions and data formats for a given machine. Same as assembly language. Contrast with *high-level language*.

```
                 START    256
        BEGIN    BALR     15,0
000102           USING    *,15
                 L        3,OLDOH
                 A        3,RECPT
                 S        3,ISSUE
                 ST       3,NEWOH
                 SVC      0
        OLDOH    DC       F'9'
        RECPT    DC       F'4'
        ISSUE    DC       F'6'
        NEWOH    DS       F
                 END      BEGIN
```

low level language

low-resolution Pertaining to the quality and accuracy of detail that can be represented by a graphics display. Resolution quality depends upon the number of basic image-forming units (pixels) within a picture image — the greater the number, the higher the resolution. Low-resolution pictures, produced by a small number of pixels, are not as sharp and clear as high-resolution pictures.

LSI See *large-scale integration*.

Mac Short for *Macintosh*.

machine language Basic language of a computer. Programs written in machine language require no further interpretation by a computer. Contrast with *source language*.

MACHINE LANGUAGE CODING FORM			
Oper	OP 1	OP 2	Comments
100010	000 000 000 000 011	010 110 100 000 000	Load register with C
001100	000 000 000 000 011	011 010 000 000 000	Multiply by B
011100	000 000 000 000 011	010 101 011 000 000	Add A
010111	000 000 000 000 011	100 001 000 000 000	Store as D

machine language

Macintosh A series of popular microcomputers from Apple Computer, Inc., first introduced in 1984. It uses the Motorola 68000 family of microprocessors, the Power PC chip, and a proprietary operating system that simulates a user's desktop on screen. This standard user interface, combined with its built-in QuickDraw graphics language, has provided a visual, easy-to-use microcomputer. The Macintosh uses a mouse as a primary input device, in addition to a keyboard. Since the introduction of the Macintosh, Apple Computer, Inc. continues to offer progressively faster and more powerful models of the Macintosh.

macro Single, symbolic programming language statement that, when translated, results in a series of machine-language statements.

magnetic disk Disk made of rigid material (hard disk) or heavy Mylar (floppy disk). The disk surface is used to hold magnetized data, which is written on the disk and retrieved from the disk by a disk drive.

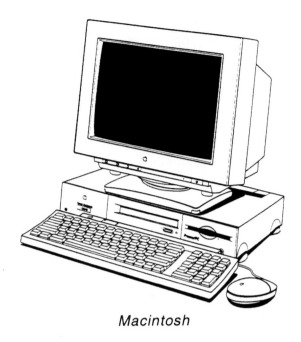

Macintosh

magnetic ink character recognition (MICR) Recognition, by machines of characters printed with a special magnetic ink. Used primarily in the banking, credit card, and public utilities industries.

magnetic media Generic name for floppy disks, tapes, and any other devices that store data in the form of magnetic impulses.

magnetic tape A plastic tape that has a magnetic surface. This surface is used to store information in a code of magnetized spots. Magnetic tape is stored on reels and cassettes.

Mahon, Charles (1753-1816) Mahon, the 3rd Earl of Stanhope, was an English statesman, scientist, and prolific inventor. He invented three calculating machines, all of which were intended primarily for performing multiplication and division by repeated addition and subtraction. The first machine was invented in 1775. In 1777, Mahon's second machine used a cam plate to bring a variable number of teeth into action. His last machine, invented in 1790, was an improvement of Samuel Morland's calculating machine. This machine was called the Stanhope Demonstrator.

Charles Mahon

mail-merging Process of automatically printing form letters with names and addresses from a mailing list file. A mail-merge program merges address information from one file with textual information from another file.

mailbox See *electronic mail.*

mainframe Large, expensive computer generally used for information processing in large businesses, colleges, and organizations. Originally, the phrase referred to the extensive array of large rack and panel cabinets that held thousands of vacuum tubes in early computers. Mainframes can occupy an entire room and have very large data-handling capacities. Far more costly than microcomputers or minicomputers, mainframes are the largest, fastest, and most expensive class of computers. Supercomputers are the largest, fastest and most expensive of the mainframes. Before minicomputers became popular in 1965, all computers were mainframes.

mainframe

main memory Refers to the Random Access Memory (RAM) of computers, where all the programs and data are stored while they are being processed or used. Main memory is also called *internal memory.*

male connectors Referring to connectors, ones that have pins or protruding parts rather than sockets or receptacles. Contrast with *female connectors.*

malfunction A failure in the operation of the computer or some other device.

138

Maltron keyboard An alternate keyboard layout that allows potentially much faster speeds, and is easier to learn than the traditional QWERTY keyboard layout. See *Dvorak keyboard* , and *QWERTY keyboard*.

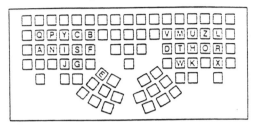

Maltron keyboard

management information system (MIS) Any information system designed to supply organizational managers with the necessary information needed to plan, organize, staff, direct, and control the operations of the organization.

Mandelbrot, Benoit B. A mathematician who invented the terms fractal and fractal geometry. Mandelbrot is an IBM Fellow at the Thomas J. Watson Research Center and a visiting professor at Harvard University. Fractal geometry lends itself to a computer solution and many programs are available to produce the complex and delicate fractal graphics. See *fractals*.

Benoit Mandelbrot

Mandelbrot set The Mandelbrot set is probably the most well-known fractal. Originally, the Mandelbrot set was discovered by Benoit Mandelbrot when he was investigating the behavior of the iterated function

$$Z_n = Z^2_{n-1} + C$$

where both Z and C are complex numbers. Mandelbrot developed a new way of mapping this equation: the Mandelbrot set. See *fractal*.

margin Number of spaces between the right or left edge of a page (or window) and the beginning of text.

marquee A rectangular area surrounded by dotted lines, used to select objects or selected portions of an image in a drawing or painting program.

Mark 1 Completed in 1944 by Harold Aiken of Harvard University and the IBM Corporation, the Mark 1, also called the Automatic Sequence Controlled Calculator, was the first large-scale electromechanical computer. See *Aiken, Howard*.

math coprocessor A special chip added to a computer to handle advanced mathematic functions, thereby freeing up the processing power of the main central processing unit. The chip performs floating point operations at high speed. In a microcomputer, it's a single chip that plugs into a special receptacle on the motherboard.

Mauchly, John (1907-1980) Co-inventor of ENIAC, the first large-scale all-electronic computer. In the 1930s, while head of the Physics Department at Ursinus College in Pennsylvania, Mauchly began experimenting with computers and electronics. In 1941, he joined the Moore School of Electrical Engineering at the University of Pennsylvania, where he met J. Presper Eckert. In early 1943, the two men submitted a proposal to the U.S. Army describing an electronic computer; the Army's Ordnance Department later issued a contract to them to build the machine. The Army needed calculated tables that would indicate to its artillerymen how to aim new guns being developed for World War II. The Moore School had been calculating

John Mauchly

these tables, but with methods that were proving too slow. Between 1943 and 1946, Eckert and Mauchly developed the Electronic Numerical Integrator And Computer, a landmark leading to the development of many future computer designs. Following the development of ENIAC, Eckert and Mauchly established their own company. They developed a second computer in 1949 called BINAC (BINary Automatic Computer), which served as a test of the plans they had formulated for UNIVAC I, the world's first general-purpose commercial computer. In 1951, UNIVAC I was installed at the U.S. Census Bureau. The corporation formed by Eckert and Mauchly is now part of Unisys Corporation, a large manufacturer of computing equipment. See *Eckert, J. Presper* and *ENIAC*.

maximize To zoom or enlarge a window so that it fills the display screen.

Mb An abbreviation for *Megabyte*. One Mb is approximately one million bytes.

McCarthy, John In 1958, created the programming language LISP. Also developed the concept of interactive computing and coined the term artificial intelligence (AI). Best known for his work associated with artificial intelligence. McCarthy taught courses in AI at both Stanford University and the Massachusetts Institute of Technology. He believes the level of interest in artificial intelligence is increasing all the time. McCarthy is currently working on nonmonotonic methods that are aimed at helping computers "reason" more like humans.

John McCarthy

mechanical mouse A mouse that uses a rubber ball that makes contact with several wheels inside the unit. Contrast with *optical mouse*.

media The plural of medium.

media interchangeability The extent to which disks recorded on one machine can play back on another with the same type of drive. Media interchangeability is excellent for floppy disks, but some removable cartridge hard disks have problems with it.

medium Any physical substance upon which data are recorded, such as floppy disk, magnetic disk, magnetic tape, CD-ROM, and paper.

medium-scale integration (MSI) Process of placing between 100-3000 electronic components on a single chip. See *integrated circuit*.

megabyte One million or 1,049,576 bytes or characters. It is also written as MB, Mb, Mbyte, M-byte and meg.

megaflop A measure of computing speed, equal to one million floating-point notation calculations per second. Abbreviated MFLOP.

megahertz One million cycles per second. Abbreviated MHz.

membrane keyboard A keyboard constructed of two thin plastic sheets (called membranes) that are coated with a circuit made of electrically conductive ink. The keyboard is sensitive to touch. It is an economical, flat keyboard used in several early microcomputers. Today such keyboards are used primarily on printers and special keyboards.

memory Storage facilities of the computer, capable of storing vast amounts of data. See *floppy disk, hard disk,* and *random access memory (RAM).*

memory address A name, letter or number that identifies a specific location where information is stored in a computer's memory.

memory capacity The maximum number of storage locations in a computer memory.

memory chip A semiconductor device used to store information in the form of electrical charges. There are two types of memory chips: ROM holds information permanently while RAM holds it temporarily. Memory is often added to a computer simply by plugging RAM chips into sockets.

memory management Technique of efficiently controlling and allocating memory resources.

memory map A diagram that shows how memory is used. For example, in a display unit there is a memory map of the screen display, with one memory location corresponding to each character position on the display.

menu A list of command options available to the user of a computer software program. An on-screen list of command choices.

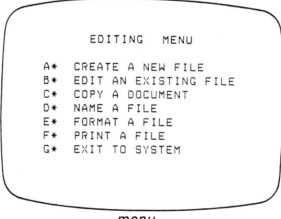

```
          EDITING   MENU

     A*   CREATE A NEW FILE
     B*   EDIT AN EXISTING FILE
     C*   COPY A DOCUMENT
     D*   NAME A FILE
     E*   FORMAT A FILE
     F*   PRINT A FILE
     G*   EXIT TO SYSTEM
```

menu

menu bar A horizontal menu at the top of a display screen or window. See *pull-down menu.*

menu-driven software Computer programs that make extensive use of menus. Software of this type is designed so it may be used easily by people with minimal computer experience. Menus are used to select tasks to be performed.

metaphor In software development, the use of words or pictures to suggest a resemblance. For example the Apple Macintosh computer uses a desktop metaphor with its icons for paper, files, folders, wastebaskets, and so on.

MFLOPS Abbreviation for Million FLoating point Operations Per Second. Used as a rough measure of a computer's processing speed.

MHz See *megahertz*.

mickey Unit of mouse movement typically set at 1/200th of an inch.

Micral The first microcomputer in the world was French. At the end of 1971, Francois Gernelle, an engineer with R2E, designed it to respond to the French agricultural research institute's need for automatic regulation. R2Es management was won over by the invention and decided to manufacture computers built around a single microprocessor. This microcomputer was called Micral. R2E was later bought out by Bull.

micro Prefix meaning one millionth, or in a more general sense, just meaning very small, as in microchip or microcomputer.

microchip A popular nickname for the integrated circuit chip. See *integrated circuit*.

microcomputer The smallest and least expensive class of computer. Any small computer that uses a microprocessor as its central processing unit (CPU). The terms microcomputer and personal computer are synonymous.

microcomputer

143

microfloppy disk A 3.5-inch floppy disk, which in recent years has become the disk of choice. The 3.5-inch disk holds more data and is much easier to store, transport and handle than its 5.25-inch counterpart. The microfloppy disk was developed by Sony.

microframe Developed in 1989, the Microframe contains a processor called SCAMP (Single Chip A Mainframe Processor) that contains as many circuits as a minicomputer, over 10 million transistors in four square inches. Microframe was originally designed as a microcomputer, and is in fact very like one, while having the power of a minicomputer.

microprocessor The complex chip that is the central processing unit (CPU) of the computer. The job of the microprocessor is to control what goes on inside the computer. All processing that a computer does takes place in the microcoprocessor. Following court proceedings lasting 20 years, the U.S. Patent Office, on July 17, 1990 recognized Gilbert Hyatt as the inventor of the microprocessor. His patent, deposited in December 1970, was the first to refer to a unique integrated circuit that contained all the necessary elements for the computer. Prior to the court's decision, the invention had been attributed to Marcian E. Hoff, Federico Faggin and Stanley Mazor of Intel Corporation. These engineers did create the first commercial microchip in history in 1971 — the Intel 4004 — however their patents were related to particular aspects of the invention, but not to its general concept.

microprocessor

microprogram A sequence of microinstructions. Microprograms are mainly used to implement machine instructions.

microsecond One millionth of a second.

Microsoft Corporation A leading software company founded in 1975 by William H. Gates and Paul G. Allen. The company's first product was Microsoft BASIC for the Altair 8800 microcomputer. Following products include MS-DOS, Microsoft Windows, Microsoft Word, Microsoft Works, GW-BASIC, QBASIC, WuickBASIC, Visual BASIC, as well as many other software systems. Microsoft's position as the supplier of the major software to the world's largest computer base (IBM-compatible microcomputers) gives it considerable influence over the future of the computer industry. See *Gates, William H.* and *Allen, Paul G.*

Microsoft Excel A spreadsheet from Microsoft Corporation for the Apple Macintosh and IBM-compatible microcomputer systems. The program provides a wide variety of business graphics and charts and takes full advantage of using laser printers for making presentation materials. Excel incorporates some of the features of page layout programs.

Microsoft Windows A graphics-based operating environment for IBM-compatible microcomputers from Microsoft Corporation. It runs in conjunction with DOS. Some of the graphical user interface features include pull-down menus, multiple typefaces, desk accessories, and the capability of moving text and graphics from one program to another via a clipboard.

Microsoft Word A full-featured word processing program for IBM-compatible microcomputers and Apple Macintosh computers from Microsoft Corporation. It has a spelling checker, hyphenation, style sheets, a glossary, mail merge, automatic text wrap, and a column design feature.

Microsoft Works An integrated application program that includes a spreadsheet, a database, and a word processor. It provides desktop publishing with drawing and word processing documents. The drawing tools and linked columns of the desktop publishing section let you create professional style layouts.

MIDI Acronym for Musical Instrument Digital Interface, a protocol for the exchange of information between computers and musical devices such as synthesizers.

migration (1) When computer users move from one hardware platform to another. (2) The process of moving data from one computer system to another without converting the data.

millisecond A thousandth of a second.

minicomputer A class of computers with capabilities and a price between microcomputers and mainframes. In 1959, Digital Equipment Corporation (DEC) launched the minicomputer industry with its PDP-1. In 1965, DEC introduced the PDP-8, the first popular, low cost minicomputer. In 1970, DEC introduced the PDP-11, which became the most widely used minicomputer in the world. Data General Corporation, Hewlett-Packard

Company, Prime Computer, Inc., IBM Corporation, and other companies have produced a variety of minicomputers.

minifloppy A 5.25-inch diskette, introduced by Shugart in 1978.

MIPS Acronym for one Million Instructions Per Second. A measure of the processing speed of a computer. Used to describe the average number of machine language instructions a mainframe or microcomputer performs in one second. For example, a computer capable of 0.5 MIPS means it can execute 500,000 instructions per second.

mode (1) An operational state that a system has been switched to. (2) Form of a number, name, or expression. (3) Most common or frequent value in a group of values.

modem Acronym for MOdulator/DEModulator, a device that translates digital pulses from a computer into analog signals for telephone transmission, and analog signals from the telephone into digital pulses the computer can understand. Provides communication capabilities between computer equipment over common telephone facilities.

modification A change to a computer software program.

modulation In data communications, the process by which some characteristic of a high-frequency carrier signal is varied in accordance with another, lower-frequency "information" signal. Used in data sets and modems to make computer terminal signals compatible with communications facilities.

Modula-2 A high-level, programming language similar to Pascal. Modula-2 supports separate compilation of modules, whereas Pascal does not. Modula-2 is very popular as a teaching language at colleges and universities.

module (1) One logical part of a program. A major program may be broken down into a number of logically self-contained modules. These modules may be written (and possibly tested separately) by a number of programmers. The modules can then be put together to form the complete program. This is called modular programming. (2) Interchangeable plug-in item containing components. (3) A set of logically related statements that perform a specific function.

moire pattern (1) An interference pattern created when two regular dot patterns are asymmetrically superimposed. (2) An undesirable grid pattern that may occur when a bit-mapped graphic with gray fill patterns is reduced

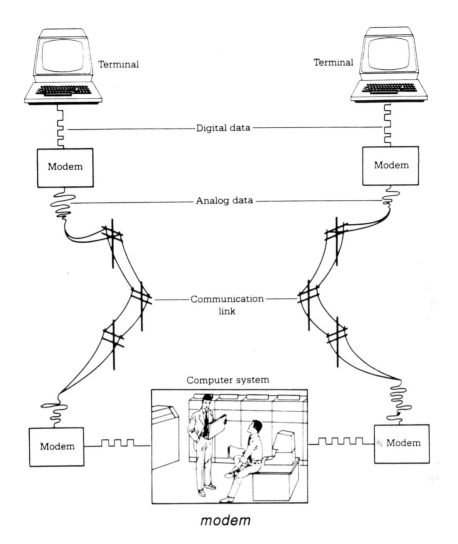

modem

or enlarged. (3) In scanning, an objectionable pattern caused by the interference of halftone screens. Often produced when you rescan a halftone and a second screen is applied on top of the first.

monitor (1) A device on which images generated by the computer's video adapter are displayed. (2) Control program or supervisor.

monitor

monochrome display A video display capable of displaying only one color. It generally has a higher resolution than a color monitor and is often more suitable for word processing and information processing, which require long periods of user viewing.

morphing A special graphics effect that makes an image look like it is transformed into another image.

Monroe, Jay R. In 1911, using earlier designs of Frank Baldwin, developed the first keyboard rotary machine to attain commercial success.

Morland, Samuel (1625-1695) Morland designed three different types of calculators. In 1663 he built a trigonometrical calculating machine, and in 1666 a calculator that was much like Pascal's calculator, except that it was pocket sized. Morland went on to invent a multiplying and dividing machine that functioned on the same principle as Napier's bones except that the tables were on rotatable disks instead of strips.

Samuel Morland

motherboard Interconnecting assembly into which printed circuit cards, boards, or modules are connected. Main circuit board of a microcomputer.

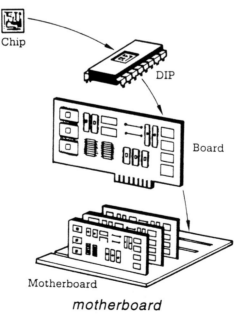

motherboard

148

Motorola, Inc. A leading manufacturer of semiconductor devices. Although the company produces many consumer electronics products, they are best known in the computer business as the manufacturer of the 68000 family of microprocessors.

Motorola 68000 family A family of microprocessors developed by Motorola, Inc: MC 68000 (a 16-bit processor) developed in 1979, MC 68010 (a 16-bit processor) developed in 1983, MC 68020 (a 32-bit processor) developed in 1984, MC 68030 (a 32-bit processor) developed in 1987, MC 68040 (a 32-bit processor) announced in 1987. The MC 68000 family of microprocessors is used in several popular microcomputers including the Apple Macintosh, Commodore Amiga, and Atari ST.

mouse A hand-operated pointing device that senses movements as it is moved across a flat surface and conveys this information to the computer. The mouse also has one or more buttons that can be pressed to signal the computer. The mouse's main advantage is that it can move a cursor around on the display screen, including diagonally, with great precision. See *mechanical mouse* and *optical mouse*.

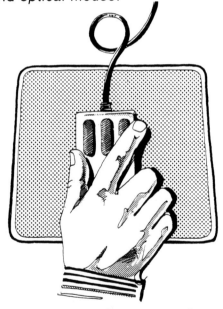

mouse and mouse pad

mouse pad A surface to be used with a mouse. As you move the mouse across the mouse pad, the cursor moves across the screen in the same direction.

mouse pointer The on-screen icon or cursor, the movement of which is controlled by the mouse.

MS-DOS Acronym for MicroSoft-Disk Operating System, the standard operating system for IBM compatible microcomputers. MS-DOS was created by Microsoft Corporation and released in 1981. MS-DOS oversees such operations as disk input and output, video support, keyboard control, and many internal functions related to program execution and file maintenance.

MSI See *medium-scale integration*.

multimedia A new technology combining computers, video, and audio technology into one interactive package.

multiprocessor A computer capable fo running more than one program at the same time, for the same or different users.

multitasking The running of two or more programs in one computer at the same time.

multiuser Two or more users sharing a single computer system at the same time.

nano A prefix indicating one billionth.

nanosecond A billionth of a second. Used to measure the speed of logic and memory chips. Light travels approximately one foot per nanosecond.

Napier, John (1550-1617) Scottish aristocrat who made many contributions to mathematics and computing. His invention of logarithms provided science and mathematics with a vastly improved and rapid method of notation and calculation. Napier tried to mechanize the use of logarithms by the manipulation of calculating rods. These were called "Napier's bones" and achieved a certain fame, but were completely outclassed and replaced by the slide rule first constructed by William Oughtred.

John Napier

National Computer Graphics Association (NCGA) Nonprofit organization dedicated to developing, promoting, and improving computer graphics applications in business, government, science, and the arts. NCGA brings together users and producers of computer graphics technology in a common, independent forum to share experience and knowledge.

natural language (1) The fifth generation of programming languages. These languages use human languages such as English, German or French to give people a more natural connection with computers. (2) Ordinary human language; unlike precisely defined computer languages, it is often ambiguous and is thus interpreted differently by different hearers.

near letter quality Not quite electric typewriter quality print from a dot matrix printer.

nest A nest occurs when one program structure is placed inside another structure of the same type. For example, a loop can be contained in another loop.

NetWare A local area network operating system developed for IBM Personal Computers and Apple Macintosh computers.

network (1) When two or more computers are connected to allow them to share the same software and information. Used primarily in businesses and schools. (2) System of interconnected computer systems and terminals. (3) Structure of relationships among a project's activities, tasks, and events. (4) A means of organizing data in artificial intelligence systems. A type of knowledge representation in artificial intelligence. (5) A system of computers, and often peripherals such as printers and scanners, linked together. See *bus network, ring network* and *star network*.

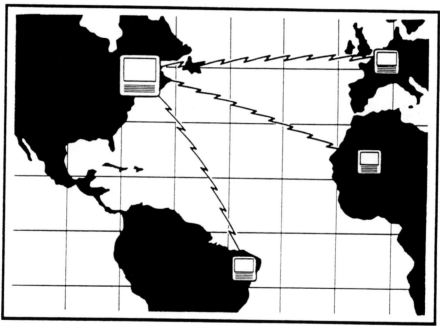

network

network administrator The person responsible for maintaining local area networks and assisting users.

network interface card (NIC) A printed circuit board that plugs into a computer, contains the circuitry and connectors that permit the computer to connect to the network.

network operating system The software that works with the network hardware to enable communications among the elements of a network.

network protocol The rules and signals that networked computers use to communicate.

network topology The geometric arrangement of nodes and cable links in a local area network. See *bus network, network, ring network,* and *star network.*

neural network (1) A computer simulation of the human brain. (2) Self-organizing systems of simple interconnected processing units which possess a learning rule and are capable of learning.

Newton A pocket-sized, pen-based computer introduced by Apple Computer, Inc. in 1992. Newton combines electronic calendar, card index, notetaking and telecommunications functions.

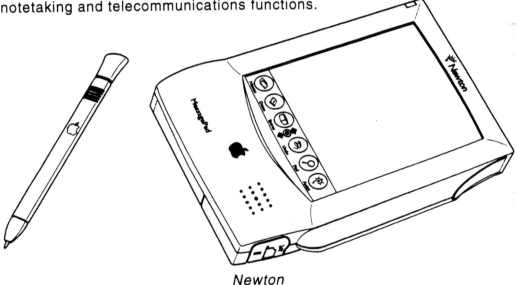

Newton

NeXT Computer A UNIX-based computer system introduced in 1988 by NeXT, Inc. It includes a Motorola 68030 microprocessor, high-resolution graphics and an erasable optical disk. NeXT, Inc. was founded in 1985 by Steven Jobs, co-founder and former chairman of Apple Computer, Inc. In 1994, NeXT, Inc. ceased the manufacturing of the NeXT Computer.

NiCad battery pack An abbreviation for Nickel Cadmium, a battery pack used for many portable computers.

node (1) Any terminal, computer or peripheral in a computer network. (2) Point in a tree structure where two or more branches come together. (3) Connecting point on a component, printed circuit board, or logic element where electrical connections can be made. (4) In computer graphics, an endpoint of a graphical element.

noise Irrelevant data that hamper the recognition and interpretation of the data of interest.

nonimpact printer Printer that uses electricity, heat, laser technology, or photographic techniques to print output. A printer that prints without striking the paper. Contrast with *impact printer*.

Norris, William C. (born 1911) In 1946, Norris launched Engineering Research Associates, which was bought by Remington Rand six years later. After Remington Rand and Sperry merged in 1955, Norris became vice-president and general manager of Univac operations. Norris, along with Seymour Cray and seven others founded Control Data Corporation (CDC) in 1957. The first computer produced by CDC was the CDC 1604, a large scientific computer. CDC went on to develop several other scientific computers: CDC 160, CDC 3600, CDC 6600, CDC 7600 and the CYBER line of mainframes. Norris guided the operations of CDC until his retirement in 1986.

William Norris

Norton Utilities A package of utility programs for IBM-compatible microcomputers, including a benchmark program that measures a computer's throughput, an undelete program that restores files accidently deleted from the disk, management utilities for directories and subdirectories, and data security programs.

notebook computer A small, self-contained, portable computer that will fit in an attache case. It usually weighs less than seven pounds and is smaller than a laptop computer.

notebook computer

Noyce, Robert Norton (1928-1990) Co-inventor of the integrated circuit, cofounder of Intel Corporation, and president of Sematech. Noyce was only 32 when he and Jack Kilby simultaneously and independently developed the integrated circuit, putting multiple transistors on a single piece of silicon and replacing roomsized computers with a chip the size of a fingernail. Noyce was so widely respected for his scientific achievements — he held 16 computer chip patents — that he became known as "The Mayor of Silicon Valley." See *Kilby, Jack.*

Robert Noyce

number crunching (1) The rapid processing of large quantities of numbers. Number crunching can be repetitive, mathematically complex, or both, and involves considerable internal processing. Parallel processing and the use of math coprocessors greatly enhance the ability of computers to perform these tasks. (2) A computer-based calculation performed by electronic spreadsheets.

numerical control Controlling a machine or process by means of digitally encoded numeric data. The control information can be prerecorded or the equipment can be under the direct control of a computer.

numeric coprocessor A microprocessor support chip that performs mathematical computations in conjunction with the main microprocessor of a system. It works in tandem with another central processing unit to increase the computing power of a system.

numeric keypad A separate section of the keyboard that contains keys for typing numbers. The keypad contains the digits 0 to 9 and a decimal point key.

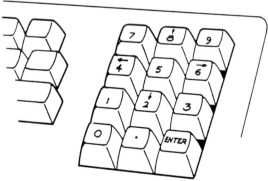

numeric keypad

object (1) In computer graphics, a distinct entity. For example, a polygon might be an object in a graphics program. (2) A shorthand term for object code. (3) In object-oriented programming, a variable comprising both routines and data that is treated as a discrete entity. The primitive element in object-oriented programming. Something you can do things to. An object has state, behavior, and identity; the structure and behavior of similar objects are defined in their common class.

object code Program instructions in a form that the computer can act on directly; machine language.

object linking and embedding (OLE) A set of standards that you use to create dynamic, automatically updated links between documents. OLE is also used to embed a document created by one application into a document created by another.

object-oriented graphics Computer graphics that are based on the use of "construction elements" such as curves, lines, and squares. Object-oriented graphics describe an image mathematically as a set of instructions for creating the objects in the image. Object-oriented graphics enable the user to manipulate objects as entire units. Because objects are described mathematically, object-oriented graphics can also be rotated, magnified and layered relatively easily. Object-oriented graphics can usually be displayed or printed at the full resolution of the monitor or output device, offering more precision than bit-mapped images.

object-oriented graphics

object-oriented programming (OOP) A programming technology that is generally more flexible and adaptable than standard programming. Object-oriented programming lets you create procedures about objects whose exact type is not known until run time. Xerox's Smalltalk was the first object-oriented language and was used to create the graphical user interface whose derivations and imitations are so popular today. C++ is an object-oriented programming language that combines traditional C programming with object-oriented features.

OCR An abbreviation for *Optical Character Recognition*, a system of translating scanned text into a form that the computer can understand as text.

Odhner, W.T. A Swedish engineer, who in 1878 invented a pin-wheel method of adding numbers from one to nine. His patents were taken up in Germany and incorporated in the best known of all hand calculating machines, the "Brunsviga," which is used in large numbers in banks, in business offices and in mathematical laboratories. The speed with which an operator can perform the normal processes of arithmetic with one of these machines is far greater than he could ever achieve with pen and ink. Since Odhner developed his machine, many other calculating machines have used the same principle.

W.T. Odhner

OEM Acronym for Original Equipment Manufacturer, a company or organization that purchases computers and peripheral equipment for use as components in products and equipment that they subsequently sell to their customers.

offline Pertaining to equipment, devices, or persons not in direct communication with the central processing unit of a computer. Equipment not connected to the computer.

Olsen, Kenneth H. Founder, in 1957, of Digital Equipment Corporation (DEC) a computer company that challenged the IBM Corporation. With the power of the minicomputer and the perseverance of Olsen, the firm grew into a multimillion dollar business. In the early 1950s, Olsen worked with Jay Forrester on the Whirlwind Computer project and the SAGE Air Defense project. Olsen and DEC developed the minicomputer in the mid-1960s. Minicomputers were smaller and less expensive than mainframes, thus they were ideal for small business applications. Olsen established the forerunner of the Computer Museum in Boston in an effort to preserve the historical aspect of the computer industry.

Kenneth Olsen

on-line information service A service that allows you to use a computer to do a variety of activities such as shopping, making travel reservations, buying and selling stocks, sending and receiving electronic mail, accessing an encyclopedia, and other information related activities. See *America OnLine, CompuServe* and Prodigy.

online system A system in which the input data enters the computer directly from the point of origin or in which output data is transmitted directly to where it is used.

on-screen help Operating assistance for applications that appear directly on the monitor, saving you the bother of looking them up in a manual.

Opel, John In 1981, guided the IBM Corporation into the microcomputer business. Under his leadership, IBM developed the IBM Personal Computer. Opel started as a salesman with IBM in 1949. Opel eventually became president in 1974 and chief executive officer in 1981. Less cautious than his corporate predecessors, Opel authorized IBM to use computer components and software made by other companies. The payoff for his calculated risk taking resulted in $500 million worth of microcomputer sales for 1982.

John Opel

open architecture (1) A computer or operating system design for which detailed specifications are published by the manufacturer, allowing others to produce compatible hardware and software. (2) Personal computer design that allows additional circuit boards to be inserted in expansion slots inside the computer to support add ons. (3) An architecture that allows integration with other languages, conventional software programs, and graphical user interfaces.

open shop Operation of a computer facility in which most productive problem programming is performed by each problem originator rather than by a group of programming specialists.

open system A vendor-independent system that is designed to interconnect with a variety of products that are commonly available. See *closed architecture*.

operating system (OS) The master set of programs that manage the computer. Among other things, an operating system controls input and output to and from the keyboard, screen, disks, and other peripheral devices; loads and begins the execution of other programs; manages the storage of data on disks; and provides scheduling and accounting services. The OS is a master control program that runs the computer and acts as a scheduler and traffic cop. See *MS-DOS, OS/2, System 7,* and *UNIX*.

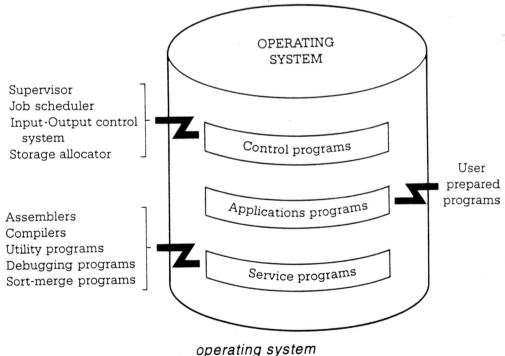

operating system

Operating System/2 (OS/2)   A multitasking operating system for IBM PC-compatible microcomputers.

optical character recognition (OCR)   Information processing technology that converts human-readable data in a special OCR font into another medium for computer input. Light reflected from characters is recognized by OCR equipment. The process by which text on paper is scanned and converted into text files in a computer.

optical computer   A type of computer, still largely experimental, that uses laser beams instead of wires to process information and works far faster than traditionally wired computers.

optical disk   A large capacity storage device. Several types of optical disks are available: CD-ROM (compact disk, read-only memory), WORM (write once, read many) and erasable optical disk drives that let you write data as well as read it. Erasable optical disks are impervious to magnetic fields and can hold data for many years. This storage technology uses a laser beam to store large amounts of data at relatively low cost.

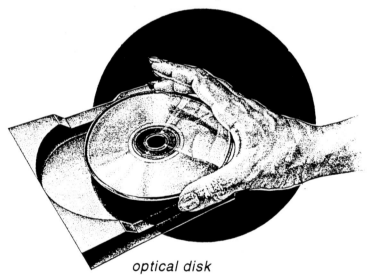

optical disk

optical disk drives   Disk drives which read or write information using light.

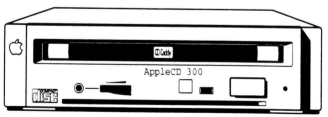

optical disk drive

optical fiber Thread of highly transparent glass that is pulsed very rapidly to carry a stream of binary signals. As well as carrying a high volume of data, optical fibers are immune to the electrical interference that can plague conventional cables. The use of optical fibers is rapidly becoming standard in computer communications.

optical mouse A mouse that uses reflected light to determine position and movement. Contrast with *mechanical mouse.*

optical mouse

optical scanner An input device that reads into the computer characters and images that are printed on a paper form.

optomechanical mouse A type of mouse in which motion is translated into directional signals through a combination of optical and mechanical means.

orientation Screen displays and printer output may appear in either of two orientations: landscape or portrait. With landscape orientation, the page is wider than it is long; with portrait orientation, the page is longer than it is wide. See l*andscape orientation* and *portrait orientation.*

original equipment manufacturer (OEM) Manufacturer who buys equipment from other suppliers and integrates it into a single system for resale.

orphan (1) First line of a paragraph sitting alone at the bottom of a page of text. Considered undesirable in all forms of printing. (2) A personal computer that has been discontinued and is no longer supported by its manufacturer.

OS Acronym for Operating System. A group of programs that control a computer and make it possible for users to enter and run their own programs. Some examples of OS are: *MS-DOS, OS/2, System 7* and *UNIX.*

OS/2 A microcomputer operating system from the IBM Corporation that allows multitasking by a single user. OS/2 was introduced in 1987. Several important OS/2 subsystems include Presentation Manager, which provides a graphical user interface, and LAN Manager, which provides networking facilities. OS/2 is designed for use on microcomputers based on Intel 80x86 processors: 80286, 80386 and 80486, and Pentium.

OS/2 Warp   A popular version of the OS/2 operating system.

Oughtred, William (1575-1660)   A mathematically minded English clergyman, in 1630 developed the earliest form of the "slide rule," two identical linear or circular logarithmic scales held together and adjusted by hand. Improvements involving the familiar inner rule with tongue-in-groove linear construction came later. The slide rule was invented to make multiplication and division easier. Oughtred was also responsible for the use of the symbol "x" for multiplication.

William Oughtred

outline font   A font that is made up of basic outlines for each character. A printer or screen font in which a mathematical formula generates each character, producing a graceful and undistorted outline of the character, which the printer then fills in at its maximum resolution. Outline fonts are available as built-in fonts in many PostScript laser printers and as downloadable fonts provided on disk.

outline font

output   The process of getting information out of a computer, or the information that comes out.

output device   Unit used for taking out data values from a computer and presenting them in the desired form to the user, such as a printer or display screen.

overflow   In an arithmetic operation, the generation of a quantity beyond the capacity of the register or storage location that is to receive the result.

overstriking   Ability of a hard-copy printer to strike a character more than once to produce special effects: boldface characters, character with a line through it, etc.

overwrite   To write data on a disk in the same area where other data is stored, thereby destroying the original data.

pack To store several short units of data into a single storage cell in such a way that the individual units can later be recovered; for example, to store two-4-bit BCD digits in one 8-bit storage location.

packet A basic unit of network communications. All communications over a network involve the sending and receiving of packets of information.

packaged software Software that is packaged and sold in stores and by mail order. The prepared package consists of the program on diskette(s), operating manual and possibly other documentation.

paddle A device for inputting information or signals to a computer. Paddles are used to play games on a computer system.

page Amount of text or graphic material displayed on a screen at one time.

page break (1) In word processing, the location where one page ends and another begins. (2) A special code placed in a document to mark the end of a page.

page composition program A program for designing and producing professional looking documents. See *desktop publishing*.

page description language (PDL) A programming language with specialized instructions for describing how to print a whole page. If an application generates output in a page description language, the output can be printed on any printer that supports it.

page design The process of specifying the boundaries of text or graphics on a page. Includes choosing margins, page length, headings and footings.

page layout program In desktop publishing, an application program that assembles text and graphics from a variety of files, with which you can determine the precise placement, scaling, sizing, and cropping of material in accordance with the page design represented on-screen. Popular page layout programs are *PageMaker, Quark XPress,* and *Ventura Publisher.*

PageMaker See *Aldus PageMaker.*

page orientation See *orientation.*

page preview A mode found on many page layout and word processing programs that shows a full-page view of how a page will look when printed out, including added elements such as headers, footers, and margins.

page printer A printer which prints a whole page as a single action. A laser printer is a page printer.

pagination (1) The integration of text, illustrations and pictures into a whole page. (2) Process of numbering or ordering pages. (3) The dividing of a document into pages.

paint program A program for creating and manipulating pixel images, as opposed to creating and manipulating object-oriented graphics. A paint program, because it treats a drawing as a group of dots (pixels), is particularly appropriate for freehand drawing. Paint programs create raster graphics images.

palette (1) Set of available colors or patterns in a computer graphics system. (2) In a paint program, a collection of drawing tools, such as patterns, colors, different line widths, brush shapes, from which the user can choose.

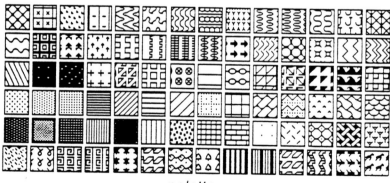

palette

palmtop computer A computer that is small enough to fit in the palm of your hand.

freehand drawing produced using a paint program

Pantone Matching System (PMS) Specific ink color specifications widely used in printing and color graphics. An extensive catalog of Pantone colors are available which describe about 500 colors; each assigned a unique PMS number. The Pantone color-selection system is supported by a variety of high-end illustration programs. A color system standardized by the Pantone Corporation.

Papert, Seymour Created the computer language LOGO with the collaboration of other computer scientists, teachers and students. Papert created LOGO in hopes that eventually children will become as comfortable with computers as they are with pencils. To carry out LOGO commands, he invented the turtle, "an object to think with." LOGO is especially well-suited to learning environments and is an excellent language to introduce students to computer programming.

Seymour Papert

Paradox A relational database management system for IBM-compatible microcomputers.

parallel Refers to something that transmits or processes several bits at a time, as opposed to serial operation, in which bits are handled one by one.

parallel port Portion of the computer through which a parallel device (such as a printer) can communicate with the computer.

parallel printer Printer that receives information from the computer one character (letter, number, etc.) at a time through eight wires. Additional wires are used to exchange control signals. A parallel printer is designed to be connected to the computer's parallel port.

parallel processing (1) The technique by which all levels of a process are carried out simultaneously. (2) A method of processing that can run only on a type of computer containing two or more processors running simultaneously. (3) A procedure that consists of the breaking down of a problem into separate components so that the computer program and the computer can work on each component of the problem simultaneously.

parameter Variable in an algebraic expression that temporarily assumes the properties of a constant. For example, in $y = mx + b$, m and b are parameters if either is treated as a constant in a family of lines.

PARC Acronym for Palo Alto Research Center. An advanced research and development arm of the Xerox Corporation which developed many of the underlying techniques for Smalltalk and graphical user interfaces.

parent File whose contents are required, and in some cases are the only sources of information available, to create new records. See *child*.

parent/child relationship Passing of information from one generation to the next. Older information (parent) is necessary to create new information (child).

parity bit Extra bit added to a byte, character, or word to ensure that there is always either an even number or an odd number of bits, according to the logic of the system. If through a hardware failure, a bit should be lost in transmission, its loss can be detected by checking the parity.

park To position a hard drive's read/write head so that the drive is not damaged while being transported.

partitioning (1) Subdividing a computer storage area into smaller units allocated to specific jobs or tasks. (2) Breaking up a problem into subtasks.

Pascal High-level structured programming language that has gained wide acceptance as a tool for both application programming and system development. Pascal was developed in the early 1970s by Niklaus Wirth. Pascal was named after the French mathematician Blaise Pascal. The language provides a flexible set of control structures and data types to permit orderly, top-down program design and development. Pascal is used extensively in the educational field for teaching programming principles and practices. See *Turbo Pascal*.

Pascaline

Pascal, Blaise (1623-1662) French mathematician who built the first desk-calculator-type adding machine in 1642. The machine, called the *Pascaline*, was made of wheels containing numbers from 0 to 9. Each wheel advanced one number when the wheel to its right completed one revolution. Pascal was an innovator in other areas as well. His inventions included the hydraulic press and the hypodermic syringe. Pascal's calculations to solve gambling problems are the basis of today's probability theory.

Blaise Pascal

passive graphics Non-interactive graphics as, for example, in the applications of instrumentation and process control — where the operator is simply receiving visual information.

password Special word, code, or symbol that must be presented to the computer system to gain access to its resources. Used for identification and security purposes on a computer system.

paste To place information previously cut from a document into a new position. With some computer systems, areas of text or graphics may be cut from a document, saved, and later pasted into another document. See *cut-and-paste*.

password catcher A program that mimics the actions of a normal sign-on screen but stores supplied ID and password combinations, usually in a hidden file accessible only to the author. The collected ID/password combinations are later used to attack the system.

patch Section of coding inserted into a program to correct a mistake or to alter the program.

pattern recognition (1) Recognition of forms, shapes, or configurations by automatic means. A subfield of artificial intelligence. (2) Using a computer to identify patterns. (3) The use of statistical techniques and templates to process and classify patterns of data. (4) In image processing, the analysis, description, identification, and classification of objects.

Patterson, John Henry Founder of the National Cash Register (NCR) Company, a manufacturer of cash registers and later, computer equipment. Patterson shaped the thinking of Thomas Watson, Sr., who later became the guiding director of the IBM Corporation. Over the years, NCR has produced a large number of computer systems. In 1991, the Intel 80x86-based System 3000 series was introduced, a complete line from laptops to large parallel processing machines.

John Patterson

PC Acronym for Personal Computer, Pocket Computer, Portable Computer, Printed Circuit, and Program Counter. The most common use of PC is to refer to IBM Corporation's Personal Computer line. Thus, for example, PC-compatible refers to a computer that can run the same programs as IBM PC or IBM PS/2 microcomputers.

PC compatibility Refers to a microcomputer that is compatible in some way with the popular IBM Personal Computer and IBM Personal System/2. Many levels of compatibility are possible.

PC-DOS Acronym for Personal Computer – Disk Operating System. IBM Corporation's trade name for its version of MS-DOS, an operating system developed and licensed by Microsoft Corporation for computers that use Intel Corporation microprocessors. There is effectively no difference between PC-DOS and MS-DOS.

PCMCIA An acronym for Personal Computer Memory Card International Association, an emerging technology for personal computers that lets a user add extra memory, a fax modem or other features without opening the machine. Instead, the circuitry is embedded on a device about the size of a credit card. The device fits a slot built into a computer.

PC Tools A software package of file and disk management utility programs for Apple Macintosh computers and IBM personal computers and compatibles.

pen computer A computer with a touch-sensitive screen and pattern recognition circuitry that can recognize human handwriting as a form of data input. The computer translates these marks into digital data and processes them as if they were typed on the keyboard.

Pentium A 64-bit microprocessor chip introduced by Intel Corporation in 1993. It can process 112 MIPS (millions of instructions per second). It is several times faster than the Intel 80486 microprocessor. Pentium is so named because it represents the fifth generation of microprocessors from Intel Corporation succeeding the popular 80486 series. The Pentium represents the continuing evolution of the 80x86 family of microprocessors.

Pentium

peripheral equipment Input/output units and auxiliary storage units of a computer system, attached by cables to the central processing unit. Used to get data in and data out, and to act as a reservoir for large amounts of data that cannot be held in the central processing unit at one time. The laser printer, hard disk and optical scanner are examples of peripherals.

personal computer (PC) The smallest and least expensive class of computer. A computer designed for use by one person at a time. Also called a *microcomputer*.

personal computer

Pet computer A low-cost, versatile computer from Commodore Business Machines, Inc., introduced in 1977. The Pet 4032 was designed for personal, educational, and scientific applications. It was one of the earliest personal computers.

PGA Acronym for Pin-Grid Array, a chip that has pins that protrude from all along the bottom of the chip.

phosphor Rare earth material used to coat the inside face of cathode ray tubes. Holds the light generated by a monitor's electron guns. Each dot on the screen is actually a phosphor that glows for a given length of time. The dots are used to create an image.

phosphor burn-in What occurs when the same image is left on the screen for extended periods of time, burning itself in so the image can be seen even when the monitor is turned off. See *screen saver*.

photo CD system A system that allows photographers to take standard 35mm pictures and have them scanned onto special compact disks at either a photofinisher or service bureau. With these disks, consumers can see their pictures on a comptuer screen. The photo CD disk format lets computer users create their own photo CD disk with combinations of photographic images, stereo audio, graphics, text and programmed access. Interactive sound and picture presentations can be created on photo CD disks for playback on computer systems.

Photoshop See *Adobe Photoshop.*

picosecond One-trillionth of a second.

PICT Acronym for PICTure file format, an object oriented graphics file format for the Macintosh computer and some programs for IBM-compatible microcomputers.

picture processing (1) In computer graphics, method for processing pictorial information by a computer system. Involves inputting graphic information into a computer system, storing it, working with it, and outputting it to an output device. (2) In artificial intelligence, the transformation of an input image into a second image, which has important properties that will help in better understanding the scene.

pie chart Graphical representation of information; charting technique used to represent portions of a whole.

pin-feed Paper-feed system that relies on a pin-studded roller to draw paper, punched with matching sprocket holes, into a printer. See *tractor feed.*

pipeline processing Overlapping operating cycle function used to increase the speed of computers. Involves decomposing a computer instruction in parts so it can be executed simultaneously. The connection of processors so that the output of one processor becomes the input of another processor.

piracy (1) Either theft, as in the appropriation of a computer design or a program, or unauthorized distribution and use of a computer program. (2) The copying and distribution of software to unauthorized users.

pitch Density of characters on a printed line, usually expressed in terms of characters per inch; for example, 10 pitch means that 10 characters are printed in every inch.

pixel Short for "picture element," a picture cell; a single dot on the computer display screen. The visual display screen is divided into rows and columns of tiny dots, squares, or cells, each of which is a pixel. Smallest unit on the display screen grid that can be stored, displayed, or addressed.

EACH PIXEL IS A DOT OF
LIGHT ON THE SCREEN

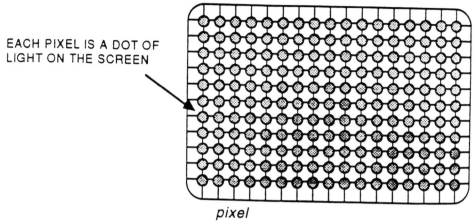

pixel

plasma display Type of visual display terminal utilizing trapped neon/ argon gas. The image is created by turning on points in a matrix (energized grid of wires) comprising the display surface. The high-resolution image is steady, long-lasting, bright, and flicker-free; selective erasing is possible.

platen A backing, commonly cylindrical, against which printing mechanisms strike to produce an impression, such as the roller in a printer against which the keys strike.

platform See *hardware platform.*

platter That part of a hard disk drive that actually stores the information. A round, flat, metallic plate covered on both surfaces with a brown magnetic substance. See *hard disk.*

plot To diagram, draw, or map with a plotter. To create an image by drawing a series of lines.

plotter An output device that draws images with ink pens. A plotter draws images as a series of point-to-point lines. Plotter types include: pen, drum, electrostatic, and flatbed.

plug compatible Peripheral device that requires no interface modification to be linked directly to another manufacturer's computer system.

PMS See *Pantone Matching System.*

pocket computer A microcomputer small enough to fit into a pocket. Pocket computers run on batteries and usually have a built-in screen.

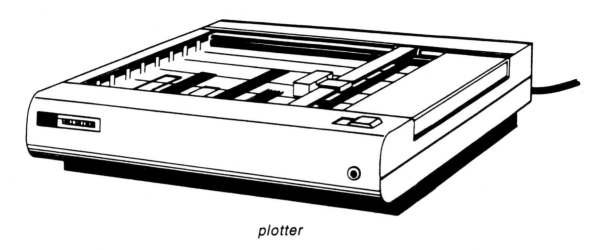

plotter

point and click To position the cursor over an object displayed on the screen (point) and press the mouse or pointing device to select it (click).

point A unit of measure used to describe the size of a font. A point is equal to 1/72 of an inch.

pointer (1) An indicator on a screen that shows where the next user computer interaction will be. Also called *cursor*. (2) Address or other indication of one storage location as held in another storage location. Used in a network database to point to related records in the same or different fields. (3) A device such as a mouse or tablet stylus that moves the cursor on the screen. (4) The additional connections in a network database between parent nodes and child nodes. (5) A variable that holds the address of another memory object.

pointer tool A tool used in layout and drawing programs to select objects or an entire block of text. It is usually represented by an on-screen arrow.

pointing device An input device, such as a mouse or graphics tablet, that is used to move the cursor on the display screen.

pointing device

173

point of sale (POS) terminal

point of sale (POS) terminal　A device used in retail establishments to record sales information in a form that can be input directly into a computer.

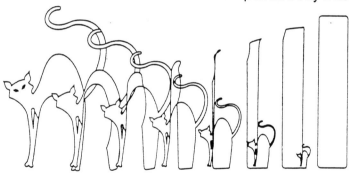

polymorphic tweening

polymorphic tweening　An animation technique that, based on information about its starting and ending shapes, creates the necessary "in-between" steps to change one object into another.

pop　In programming, to access an item from a stack and so remove it from the stack. See *push* and *stack*.

pop-up menu　A menu that appears on-screen anywhere other than in the standard menu bar location.

port　That portion of a computer through which a peripheral device may communicate. Plug-in/socket on the back of the computer for connecting cables for peripherals.

portable computer

portable computer A self-contained computer that can be easily carried and moved.

portable program A program that can be run easily on a number of different computers.

portrait monitor A monitor with a screen shape higher than it is wide. A popular type monitor in desktop publishing systems.

portrait orientation An orientation in which the data has a height greater than its width. Contrast with *landscape orientation*. See *orientation*.

portrait orientation

PostScript A proprietary language developed by Adobe Corporation to tell a printer what to print on a particular page. PostScript's chief benefit is its device independence, that is to say that the same file can be printed to printers of varying resolutions.

PostScript laser printer A laser printer that includes the processing circuitry needed to decode and interpret printing instructions phrased in PostScript — a page description language widely used in desktop publishing. The printer converts the PostScript instructions (sent by the computer) into the dots that make up the printed image.

PowerBook

PowerBook A trademark for any of a group of Apple Macintosh laptop computers first released in 1992.

power down (1) To turn off a computer or peripheral device. (2) Steps a computer may take to preserve the state of the processor and to prevent damage to it or to connected peripherals when the power fails or is shut off. Contrast with *power up*.

Power PC chip

Power PC chip A computer chip, introduced in 1994, that was developed by an IBM-Apple Computer-Motorola alliance. As computers get smaller and smaller, the costs of developing the technology behind the trend are becoming too heavy for any corporation to bear alone. Thus, companies increasingly are combining forces to share the burden. See *Intel Corporation*.

power supply A device that provides power to electronic equipment such as computers and peripherals. Power supplies are rated by wattage; the higher the wattage, the stronger the power supply.

power surge A sudden, brief increase in the flow of current that can cause problems in the proper operation of computer equipment.

power up (1) To turn on a computer or peripheral device. (2) Steps taken by a computer processor when the power is turned on, or restored after a power failure. The processor and peripherals are initialized so that program execution may be started. Contrast with *power down*.

power user A computer user who has gone beyond the beginning and intermediate stages of computer use. Such a person uses the advanced features of application programs.

PPM An abbreviation for *Pages Per Minute*, a unit of measure used to describe printer speed.

precedence Rules that state which operators should be executed first in an expression.

precision Degree of exactness with which a quantity is stated. A calculation may have more precision than accuracy: the true value of π is accurate only to about five places.

presentation graphics High quality professional looking business graphics. Used in proposals, business presentations, manuals and other business related documents. An easy-to-understand display of numerical information. Presentation graphics are visually appealing and easily understood by an audience.

Presentation Manager A graphical user interface (GUI) and application program interface (API) for OS/2. See *OS/2*.

preventive maintenance Maintenance done on a scheduled basis to prevent major problems. Involves cleaning and adjusting the equipment as well as testing the equipment, under both normal and marginal conditions.

primary storage The electronic circuitry that temporarily holds data and program instruction needed by the central processing unit. Also called memory, primary memory, main storage, internal storage and main memory.

primitive (1) The basic building blocks of a language. In the English language individual words are primitives. In this vein, keywords in BASIC or Pascal may be considered as primitives. (2) In computer graphics the most basic graphic entities available, such as points, line segments, or characters. Primitives are the elements from which large graphic designs are created. (3) Basic or fundamental unit, often referring to the lowest level of a machine instruction or the lowest unit of language translation.

printed circuit board A special board on which specific circuits have been etched or "printed."

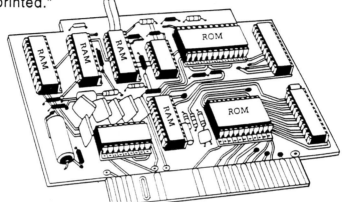

printed circuit board

printer Output device that produces hardcopy output.

printer driver A device driver used to control a printer.

printer font A font available for printing. There are three types of printer fonts: built-in fonts, cartridge fonts, and downloadable fonts.

printer port A receptacle on the back of the computer that allows you to connect a printer to the computer.

printer resolution The number of dots a laser printer can print on a linear inch. For example, most laser printers image at 300 dpi, while high-end imagesetters print at resolutions of 1270, 2540, and higher.

printout A listing or drawing produced by a printer.

print server A device that coordinates the shared printer resources of a network.

print spooling Routing jobs to be printed to a buffer, which releases them when the printer is ready to print, allowing users to continue to work on the computer while printing takes place.

178

procedure (1) Course of action taken for the solution of a problem. (2) Portion of a high-level-language program that performs a specific task necessary for the program. (3) Another name for a computer program.

process control The use of the computer to control an industrial process, such as oil refining, steel production, or electric power plant operation.

processing Computer manipulation of data in solving a problem.

processor (1) The central processing unit of a computer. (2) A computer is sometimes referred to as a language processor. (3) In addition to the central processing unit, many sophisticated computer systems contain a dedicated processor for accelerated calculations.

Prodigy An on-line information service that offers business, shopping, news, and information services. Prodigy is a partnership of IBM Corporation and Sears Roebuck and Company. Innovative features of Prodigy include the use of a bit-mapped graphical user interface and unlimited use of the system for a flat fee. See *on-line information service.*

program Series of instructions that will cause a computer to process data. It may be in a high-level source form, which requires intermediate processing before the computer can execute it, or it may be in an object form directly executable by the computer.

```
' Prints the first few odd and even numbers
CLS
PRINT "Even numbers through 20"
' Start at 2 because it's the first even number
FOR num = 2 to 20 STEP 2
    PRINT num
NEXT num

PRINT "Odd numbers below 20"
FOR num = 1 to 20 STEP 2
    PRINT num
NEXT num
```
program

program file A file which stores a program.

program library A collection of computer programs for a computer.

program maintenance The process of debugging and upgrading a program, by finding and fixing any problems, and by adding new features at the request of users.

programmer Person whose job is to design, write, and test software.

programming The process of setting up a procedure for problem solving which can be understood by a specific computer.

programming language A set of statements that control the operations of a computer. A means for computer users to provide a series of instructions for a computer to follow. There are four types of programming languages: machine language, assembly language, high-level language, and fourth-generation language.

```
TO  FILL.FD  :N
IF  :N=0  THEN  STOP
MAKE  "REALX  XCOR
MAKE  "REALY  YCOR
SETXY  :ANCHORX  :ANCHORY
SETXY  :REALX  :REALY
FD  1
FILL.FD  :N-1
END
```
programming language

PROLOG Acronym for PROgramming in LOGic, a logic-based programming language. PROLOG is widely used in programming applications such as expert systems and artificial intelligence software. It was developed in the early 1970s by Alain Colmerauer and Philippe Roussel.

PROM An acronym for Programmable Read Only Memory. It is a type of storage used in microcomputers. A PROM is not programmed during manufacturing. It requires a physical or electrical process to program it.

prompt Any message output by a computer system that requires some response from the operator.

proportional sizing A proportion is the relation, or ratio, of one part to another and of each part to the whole with regard to size, height, width, length, or depth. Most graphics programs allow you to resize and reshape graphic objects on the display screen. Proportional sizing should be used whenever you wish a scaled image to keep proper dimensions, otherwise the scaled image will be distorted.

proportional spacing If the horizontal space allotted to a printed character is proportional to the width of that character, the spacing is said to be proportional. Since this book is typeset in proportional spacing, the "w" in the word "write" consumes more space than the "i." Standard typewriter style, in contrast, allots equal space to all characters.

protocol A mutually agreed-upon procedure for the exchange of information, which allows the receiver to interpret properly the transmitted information.

PS/1 See *IBM Personal System/1*.

PS/2 See *IBM Personal System/2*.

public domain software Software not protected by copyright laws and therefore free for all to reproduce and trade without fear of legal prosecution. Any computer program donated to the public by its creator. Public domain software may be duplicated by others at will.

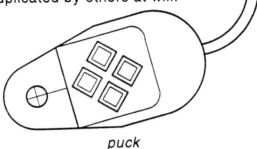

puck

puck Hand-held, manually controlled, graphics input device used to pinpoint coordinates on a digitizing tablet. Has a transparent window containing cross hairs and allows coordinate data to be digitized into the system from a drawing placed on the digitizing tablet surface.

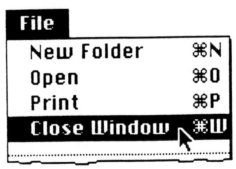

pull-down menu

pull-down menu A second-level menu, or list of commands, that appears from the top of the screen when a command needs to be given and then disappears when the selection has been made. A pull-down menu is usually used as an extension to a menu bar. To select an option on a pull-down menu, one presses and holds down the mouse button while dragging the mouse pointer down the menu until the wanted option is highlighted.

push In programming, to add an item to a stack. See *pop* and *stack*.

181

QBASIC A dialect of the BASIC programming language. A program written in QBASIC is interpreted by a QBASIC interpreter and then executed by the computer to produce the resulting output. QBASIC was developed by the Microsoft Corporation and is provided as part of the DOS (DISK OPERATING SYSTEM). QBASIC is one of the most powerful interpreted languages on the market today.

Quadra A series of high-end Macintosh computers powered by the Motorola 68040 microprocessor.

Quadra computer

Quark Xpress A page layout program for the Apple Macintosh computer from Quark, Inc. It's noted for its precise typographic control and sophisticated graphics capabilities. Quark Xpress allows unlimited document length and includes many word processing features.

Quattro Pro A popular spreadsheet for IBM-compatible microcomputers from Borland International, Inc. The program provides advanced graphics and presentation capabilities.

query To ask for information. To make a request for information from a database system.

query language A user's language for retrieving data from a database management system. A query is typically issued in the form of a sentence or near-English command.

queue A waiting line in which each item follows the other. When several jobs are waiting to be run on a computer, they are said to be "in the queue."

QuickBASIC A variation of the BASIC programing language published by Microsoft Corporation. QuickBASIC is a compiler that recognizes modern control structures and enables programmers to omit line numbers. The compiler enables you to create structured programs, complete with indentations. QuickBASIC programs execute much faster than their interpreted counterparts.

QuickDraw A graphics language system built into the ROM of the Apple Macintosh computer. Application programs call on QuickDraw for on-screen displays. QuickDraw consists of a series of primitive shapes, lines, and fill patterns which can be mathematically modified. When printing to PostScript printers, QuickDraw must be translated during the printing process by a program called a PostScript interpreter.

quit (1) To exit the current application program. (2) An action that tells a system to return to a previous state or stop a process.

QWERTY keyboard

QWERTY keyboard Keyboard arrangement that is standard on most keyboards found on typewriters, word processors, and computers. Developed more than a century ago to slow down swift typists and prevent jamming of the old mechanical typewriters. The design is called QWERTY after the first six letters on the top alphabetic line of the keyboard. Now that electronics can accommodate high-speed typing, QWERTY is no longer efficient. Many businesses are replacing QWERTY keyboards with the more efficient *Dvorak keyboard*. Some computer companies now offer keyboards with a switch that will change from one keyboard to the other. See *Dvorak keyboard* and *Maltron keyboard*.

radio button In a graphical user interface, the round option buttons that appear in dialog boxes. Only one radio button can be selected within a group of radio buttons.

ragged left alignment Refers to text printed with a straight right margin and an uneven left margin. Also called *flush right*.

ragged right alignment Text printed with a straight left margin and an uneven right margin. Also called *flush left*.

RAM Acronym for Random Access Memory, a memory into which the user can enter information and instructions (write) and from which the user can call up data (read). Working memory of the computer, into which applications programs can be loaded from outside and then executed.

RAM cache A section of random access memory (RAM) set aside to serve as a buffer between the central processing unit and the disk drive.

RAM disk An area of RAM configured by a program to emulate a disk drive.

random access Process of obtaining data from, or placing data into, a storage location in which access is independent of the order of storage.

random access memory (RAM) Memory whose contents can be read or written on directly without regard to any other memory location.

raster graphics Manner of storing and displaying data as horizontal rows of uniform grid or picture cells (pixels). Raster scan devices recreate or refresh a display screen thirty to sixty times a second to provide clear images for viewing. Raster display devices are generally faster and less expensive than vector tubes.

ray tracing In computer graphics, a method of adding a degree of realism to an image through the use of reflections, refractions, and shadows. A sophisticated and complex approach to producing high-quality computer graphics. Ray tracing is a very process-intensive operation.

read To get information from any input or file storage media, such as reading a floppy diskette by sensing the patterns of magnetism. Contrast with w*rite*.

read-only memory (ROM) Special type of computer memory, permanently programmed with one group of frequently used instructions. Does not lose its program when the computer's power is turned off, but the program cannot be changed by the user. In some microcomputers, the BASIC language interpreter and operating systems are contained in ROM.

read/write head Small electromagnet used to read, write, or erase data on a magnetic storage device, such as a disk or tape.

real-time image generation Performance of the computations necessary to update an image being completed within the refresh rate, so the sequence appears correctly to the viewer. An example is fight simulation, in which thousands of computations must be performed to present an animated image, all within the rate of 30-60 cycles per second at which the frames change.

real-time processing The manipulation of data that are required or generated by some process while the process is in operation.

reboot To stop and boot the operating system again. Usually occurs by human intervention as the result of a problem. Similar to "reset" on a home appliance. To restart.

record Collection of related items of data treated as a unit. Description of an item in a database. Each item is represented by a record that consists of one or more fields. Everyday examples of a record include an entry in a dictionary or a listing in a phone book.

recover Commonly used to describe the process of restoring lost or damaged files.

recursion The performance of an operation in several steps, with each step using the output of the preceding step.

reduced instruction set computer (RISC) A microprocessor that has only a relatively small set of instructions. RISC design is based on the premise that most of the instructions a computer decodes and executes are simple, thus RISC architecture limits the number of instructions that are built into the microprocessor but optimizes each so it can be carried out very rapidly.

reflecting chips A product of DMD (Deformable Mirror Device) technology, this chip contains a multitude of microoptic silicon mirrors mounted on pivots and activated by electric signals. Depending on its position, each mirror reflects or refracts light from its source, thus recreating part of an image. This technique, developed by Texas Instruments researchers in 1991, creates more viable, less energy consuming and compact chips. The first commercial application of this invention was for a printer to be used by travel agents.

reformat To change the representation of data from one format to another.

refreshing Process of constantly reactivating or restoring information that decays or fades away when left idle. Phosphor on a CRT screen needs to be constantly reactivated by an electron beam to remain illuminated. Typically, the image must be regenerated at a rate of 30 to 60 hertz to avoid flicker. Likewise, cells in dynamic memory elements must be repeatedly accessed to avoid losing their contents.

relational database A database that can link information from two or more separate files. Relational databases are more complex and somewhat harder to learn than regular databases.

relational operator Symbol used to compare two values; specifies a condition that may be either true or false, such as = (equal to), < (less than), and > (greater than).

release number The number that identifies a specific version of a program. A program labeled 3.5, for example, is the sixth release of Version 3 of the program (the first was Version 3.0).

remote Physically distant from a local computer, such as a terminal or printer.

remote access Being able to use a computer from a distance, usually through a modem and telephone lines.

removable hard disk A special sort of hard disk where the platters and some of the mechanism is removable.

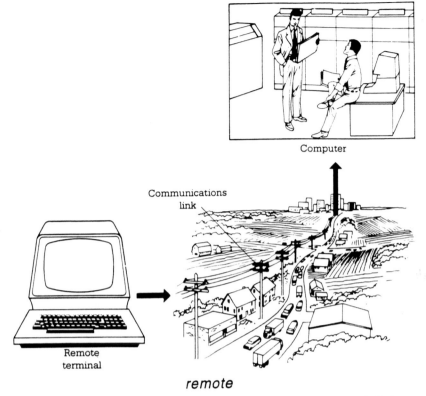

Computer

Communications link

Remote terminal

remote

removable storage Diskettes, hard disk cartridges, or optical disk cartridges that can be removed from the device that reads data from them or writes data to them.

rename To change the file name on disk.

repagination Process in which a page layout or word processing program adjusts a multipage document as it is revised to ensure uniform page length and appearance.

repeat dialer A program that continually calls the same number, thus placing it virtually out of service for any other caller.

repeat key Keyboard key that can be held down so it repeatedly makes contact without need for additional pressing.

replace In word processing, command that enables a user to search for a word and replace it with another one.

report Usually associated with output data; involves the grouping of related facts so as to be easily understood by the reader. Common means of presenting information to users. Most reports are on-screen display or printed listings showing selected information extracted from a database.

reseller Anyone who sells computer products.

reset button A button on many computers used to reboot the computer without turning off the power.

resident program Program that occupies a dedicated area of a computer's main memory (ROM or RAM) during the operating session.

resolution The resolution of a printer or display screen is a measure of the sharpness of the images it can produce.

resource Any component of a computer configuration. Memory, printers, visual displays, disk storage units, software, materials, and operating personnel are all considered resources.

response time The time it takes for a computer to respond to input from the keyboard or mouse.

retrieving Process of making stored information available when needed.

return Set of instructions at the end of a subroutine that permits control to return to the proper point in the main program.

return See *enter/return key*.

reverse print

reverse print Having white type or graphics on a black background (or some variation on that theme) instead of the usual black type or graphics on a white background.

RGB monitor A special kind of color monitor. Its display is made by three separate signals — one for each of the colors red, green and blue (RGB), which are the colors used to make a screen picture. This makes a clearer and sharper picture than one combined signal used by normal color TV.

right justification A method of aligning text so that each line of text is flush against the right margin, leaving a ragged or uneven left margin.

ring network One of the three principal topologies for a local area network, in which each computer is connected to other computers, forming a continuous loop, or circle. See b*us network, network,* and *star network.*

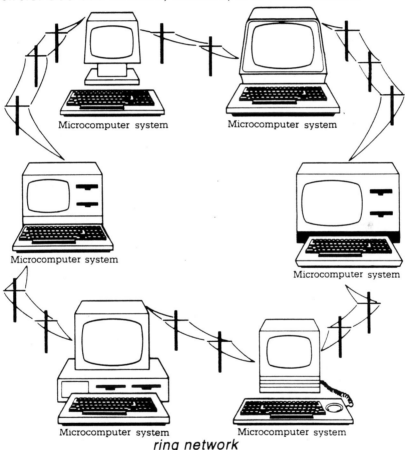

ring network

RISC Short for **R**educed **I**nstruction **S**et **C**omputer, a computer system designed to minimize the number of different underlying operations that the microprocessor does in hardware in order to optimize the execution speed. Such systems depend on the software for functions that formerly were handled by the microprocessor. RISC technology was invented by John Cocke, a research scientist at the IBM Corporation. A RISC processes information faster by concentrating on the functions most often performed.

189

Ritchie, Dennis A Bell Laboratories research scientist who, in 1971, with Kenneth Thompson, developed and implemented the UNIX operating system. The UNIX system has led a generation of software designers to new ways of thinking about programming. Ritchie also developed the C programming language.

Dennis Ritchie

Roach, John V. In 1977, Tandy Corporation's Radio Shack division released the TRS-80 microcomputer. Roach, then a vice-president at Radio Shack manufacturing, guided the development of this popular microcomputer. Roach persuaded Tandy Corporation's management to manufacture a microcomputer and market it through the Radio Shack stores. The public response to the TRS-80 was more favorable than anticipated and the sales reflected this. Tandy's Radio Shack division has become a leader in the microcomputer market. Roach became president of Tandy in 1980, chief executive officer in 1981, and chairman in 1982.

John Roach

robotics The science of robot design and use. The branch of engineering devoted to the creation and training of robots. Robots are computer-controlled devices capable of performing many of the tasks performed by humans.

ROM Acronym for Read-Only Memory. Generally, a solid state storage chip programmed at the time of its manufacture and that cannot be reprogrammed by the computer user. Also called *firmware*, since this implies software that is permanent or firmly in place on a chip.

ROM cartridge Plug-in module that contains software permanently stored in ROM. A method of entering data and/or programs into a computer. The module can contain one or more printer fonts, programs, games or other information.

root directory Under DOS, the first, top-level directory.

rotation In computer graphics, the turning of a computer-modeled object relative to an origin point on a coordinate system. In three-dimensional graphics, an object can be rotated in space, usually around the axis, to provide different views. In two-dimensional graphics, an object can revolve around a point.

rotation

row (1) Horizontal members of one line of an array. (2) Vertical divisions of an electronic spreadsheet. Together with columns, rows serve to form the spreadsheet matrix. Contrast with *column*.

RS-6000 An abbreviation for RISC System/6000, an IBM family of RISC-based workstations introduced in 1990.

run Single or continuous execution of a program by a computer on a given set of data. See *execute*.

satellite (1) A terminal or workstation linked to a centralized host computer. (2) An earth-orbiting device capable of relaying communications signals over long distances.

sans serif Letters of typefaces without serifs — the ornate, widened bases and tops seen on some characters of some type fonts. As a matter of fact, sans means "without" in French. Sans serif fonts have very clean lines and are typically considered friendly, casual and familiar.

save To store information somewhere other than in the computer's internal memory, such as on a tape or disk, so it can be used again.

scalable font Characters which can be scaled to any size via a page description language. By contrast, bitmap fonts must be loaded for every size, using up storage space. Scalable fonts provide more flexibility than bit-mapped fonts by eliminating the need to store a variety of different font sizes in the computer's memory.

scaling (1) Process of changing one bit-map density into a bit-map of another density. Scaling usually involves enlarging or contracting an image. (2) Process of changing the size of an image. Scaling by a factor of three multiplies all dimensions of an image by 3.

scanned image A bit-mapped, or TIFF (Tagged Image File Format), image generated by an optical scanner. Many layout programs can scale or crop scanned images before placing them into a page.

scanner An optical reading device that can recognize text, drawings and photographs and convert them into electronic representation of the images. Scanners can be differentiated by whether they process color or are limited to shades of gray. Scanner resolution is determined by the amount of information available from the scanning sensor for a given area. Common resolutions in desktop scanners are 300-1200 dots per inch. More powerful systems can scan up to 8000 lines per inch or more.

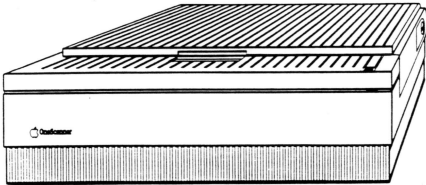

scanner

Scheutz, George (1785-1873) In 1854, twenty years after the principles of Babbage's Difference Engine were published in the Edinburgh Review, a Swedish printer and engineer named George Scheutz constructed a model of Babbage's machine. A year later, this machine won a gold medal in Paris where it was exhibited with drawings made by Charles Babbage and his son Edvard. The machine was purchased in 1856 for the Dudley Observatory in Albany, New York. A copy commissioned by the British government was completed in 1859 and used to calculate actuarial tables used for predicting life expectancy.

George Scheutz

Schickhard, Wilhelm (1592-1632) In 1624 Schickhard, a professor of mathematics and astronomy at Tubingen, Germany, wrote Kepler that he had invented a calculating machine, and a sketch by the mechanic who built the device for Schickhard has been found in the State Library in Stuttgart. A model of this device has been reconstructed; the upper register consisted of a cylindrical form of Napier's rods, and the lower portion was a stylus-operated adding mechanism providing for six digits with automatic carry.

Wilhelm Schickhard

scientific visualization Technology that enables scientists to store vast amounts of mathematical data, generate graphical models that represent the data, and visually analyze the results, usually through interactive software programs. Scientific visualization is a multidisciplinary methodology which employs the largely independent, but converging fields, of computer graphics, image processing, computer vision, signal processing, and computer-aided design. Its specific goal is to act as a catalyst between scientific computation and scientific insight. Scientific visualization came into being to meet the ever increasing need to deal with highly active, very dense data sources, which, for example include satellite data and data from supercomputer computations.

scrapbook A storage location for frequently used text and pictures. The stored images can be inserted into new documents as required.

scratch pad A high-speed memory circuit in a microprocessor, used for temporary storage of preliminary data during processing.

screen A surface on which information is displayed. An example is a video display screen.

screen capture (1) The transfer of the image on the current display screen into a graphics file. (2) A printout of the current screen display.

screen cursor An indicating symbol generated by the display hardware and moved by the user around the screen area. Its position on the screen can be made to correspond to the position of a hand-held input device, such as a mouse moved across a mouse pad.

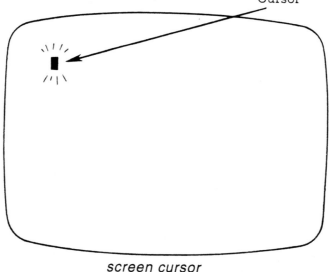

screen cursor

screen dump Process of transferring the information currently appearing on a display screen to a printer or saved as a file on disk; a "snapshot" of the screen.

screen flicker The appearance of a flicker or other distortion on a computer display screen.

screen fonts The bitmapped representations of a printer font that is used to display the font on the screen. A screen font is designed to mimic the appearance of printer fonts when displayed on medium-resolution monitors.

screen memory A portion of RAM that stores data needed to display whatever is output to the display screen.

screen resolution A measure of the crispness of images and characters on a screen, usually specified in terms of the number of pixels in a row or column.

HIGH-RESOLUTION   LOW-RESOLUTION

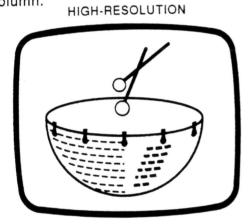 

screen resolution

screen saver A program that produces moving patterns on the screen after a specified number of minutes without keyboard or mouse activity. Pressing a key on the keyboard or moving the mouse restores the screen. Screen savers are used to prolong the life of a monitor; they prevent one image from being burned into the screen phosphors. See also *phosphor burn-in*.

scrolling The vertical or horizontal movement of information (text or graphics) on a display screen in order to display additional information.

SCSI Stands for Small Computer Systems Interface. The SCSI is a general purpose parallel interface designed for connecting one or more computers and one or more peripherals — a total of eight devices may be connected to one bus. It is an industry standard interface for high-speed access to peripheral devices. Used extensively on the Apple Macintosh computer. SCSI's great advantage is its ability to chain together multiple devices on a single I/O card, each of which has a unique address. Pronounced "scuzzy."

Sculley, John   During the first decade of its existence, Apple Computer Inc. blazed a counterculture path at the vanguard of the personal computer industry. Founders Stephen Wozniak and Steven Jobs became legends; Wozniak for engineering the Apple II and Jobs for giving the Macintosh its unusual personality. In 1983 Sculley left PepsiCo to run Apple. Two years later, after Jobs departure, Sculley introduced Apple's Macintosh Plus and LaserWriter Plus. Under Sculley's guidance, Apple introduced many other new Macintosh models and associated products. After a decade of guidance by Sculley, Apple Computer has become a major computer corporation. Scully left Apple in 1993.

John Sculley

search   To look for data in a file, usually a database, in which the object is to find all of the records that meet certain criteria.

search and replace   Software feature that finds a designated character sequence and replaces it with a new one. Important in word processing applications.

secondary storage device   A machine, such as a disk unit, mass storage device, tape unit, capable of providing storage to supplement primary memory.

second generation computers   Computers belonging to the second era of technological development of computers, when the transistor replaced the vacuum tube. Prominent from 1959 to 1964, when they were displaced by computers using integrated circuitry.

sector   The smallest unit of storage on a disk. Disks are divided into sectors and tracks. The address where data is stored is made up of the sector and track number.

security   State achieved by hardware, software, or data as a result of successful efforts to prevent damage, theft, or corruption.

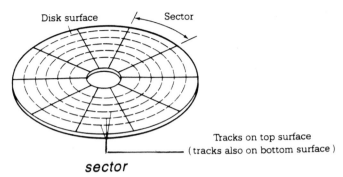

Disk surface — Sector

Tracks on top surface
(tracks also on bottom surface)

sector

seek To position the access mechanism of a direct access device at a specified location.

seek time The time it takes to move the read or write head of a disk drive to a particular track on the disk.

semiconductor A material such as silicon, used in making integrated circuits for computers.

serial Any set of things arranged in a row, one after another, are in a series, or in serial form.

serial communications Method of data transfer in which the bits composing a character are sent sequentially. Required for telephone data transfer.

serial mouse A mouse that connects to a computer's serial port.

serial port Input/output port in a computer through which data are transmitted and received one bit at a time.

serial printer Printer that receives information from the computer one bit at a time through a single wire. (One character equals eight bits). One or more additional wires may be necessary to exchange control signals. Prints one character at a time. Serial printers are designed to be connected to the computer's serial port.

serif An ending stroke on the arms, tails and stems of characters in certain typeface designs. Serif type styles are typically considered businesslike, formal, and authoritative.

A SERIF TYPEFACE   A SANS SERIF TYPEFACE
TIMES ROMAN AVANT GARDE

serif

server In the client/server model for a network system, the server is a machine with computer resources and large memory capacity.

service bureau An organization that provides data processing services, business software development or pre-press services to its customers.

Shannon, Claude E. (born 1916) Made contributions to Boolean algebra, cryptography, computing circuits, and to communications with his mathematical theory of information. His ideas were important in the development of the binary system of information storage on which the modern computer is based. His ideas gave impetus to the field of information theory. It has proved useful not only in circuit design, computer design, and communications technology; it is being applied to biology and psychology, to phonetics, and even to semantics and literature.

Claude Shannon

shareware Software that is passed around. The authors let you copy and share their programs freely, but retain the copyrights. Shareware provides income to its author in the form of "contributions," much like public TV. Payment is strictly voluntary. Even though shareware is given away free, the maker hopes that satisfied users will voluntarily pay for it.

sharpness Clarity and quality of an image produced on a visual display device, digital plotter, printer, film recorder, and other devices. See *resolution*.

sheet feeder Device that attaches to the printer, designed to automatically insert and line up single sheets of paper or envelopes in much the same way as an operator would perform the task. Usually sits above the printer platen and is operated either mechanically or electrically by the printer.

shell An operating environment layer that separates the operating system from the user. The shell provides a graphical icon-oriented or menu-driven interface to the system in order to make it easier to use. See *kernel*.

shift key The keyboard key you press to enter uppercase letters or punctuation marks.

Shockley, William Bradford (1910-1989)
Shockley shared the 1956 Nobel Prize for physics with John Bardeen and Walter Brattain for their work at Bell Laboratories in developing the transistor, a device providing the underpinning for many innovations in electronics. After leaving Bell Labs in 1954, Shockley organized a semiconductor company that led to the development of California's Silicon Valley. Employees who went their independent ways after first working for him were later involved in developing the integrated circuit and microprocessors.

William Shockley

shrink-wrapped software   A ready-to-use software product that is packaged and ready for sale.

shrink-wrapped software

SIGGRAPH   A special interest group on computer graphics that is part of the Association for Computing Machinery (ACM). Each year SIGGRAPH holds an annual conference. The conference has become a focus for the exchange of information regarding fundamental discoveries and the latest innovations in the field of computer graphics The conference includes lectures, exhibits, films and a computer art show.

silicon   An element used in the manufacture of integrated circuits. Next to oxygen, silicon is the most abundant element in the earth's crust. Semiconductors are made from refined beach sand, which is mostly silicon, melted and transformed into giant crystals. These are then sawed into thin wafers imprinted with the hundreds of copies of the diagrams needed to make integrated circuits, and then cut up into the tiny individual chips that go into computers and other devices.

Silicon Valley   Nickname for an area south of San Francisco noted for its large number of electronic, semiconductor, and computer manufacturing firms. Also known as Silicon Gulch.

SIMM An acronym for Single Inline Memory Module, a tiny printed circuit board to which several memory chips are attached. It plugs into a slot on a larger printed circuit board and is handled as if it were a single integrated circuit chip.

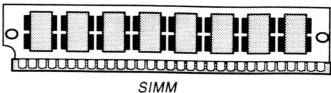

SIMM

simplex A data line that transmits data in only one direction.

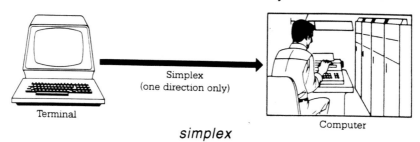

simplex

simulation Representation of certain features of the behavior of a physical or abstract system by the behavior of another system, such as the representation of physical phenomena by means of operations performed by a computer, or the representation of operations of a computer by those of another computer.

single density Method of storing data on a diskette. See *double density*.

Single In-line Memory Module (SIMM) A module designed to add memory to a computer system. SIMMs are used in the Apple Macintosh line of computers.

single-sided disk Diskette with only one side used for reading and writing information. Contrast with *double-sided disk*.

single user One person at one time using a computer.

SIP Acronym for Single In-line Package, a package that has one row of chips in a straight line.

site license License permitting a customer to make multiple copies of a piece of software and distribute them freely within the facility.

slot A socket in a computer designed to accept a plug-in circuit board.

Small Computer System Interface See *SCSI*.

small-scale integration (SSI) Process of placing less than 100 electronic components on a single chip. See *integrated circuit*.

smart system In communications, any system utilizing artificial intelligence technology.

smoothing A technique used for eliminating jaggies, the jagged distortions that appear on curves.

softcopy Information presented as a video image, in audio format, or in any other form that is not hardcopy.

soft font A font that is downloaded from a computer to a printer from files stored on a disk.

soft hyphen Conditional (nonrequired) hyphen printed only to break a word between syllables at the end of a line. Contrast with *hard hyphen*.

soft page break In word processing, a page break inserted by the program.

soft return Combination line feed/carriage return command, entered by a program containing the word wrap feature to begin a new line within a paragraph. Unlike a hard return, it is conditional — the computer executes the command only when the current word doesn't fit in the line in progress.

software The generic term for any computer program or programs; instructions that cause the hardware to do work. Contrast with the "iron" or hardware of a computer system.

software developer A person or firm that develops and markets software for profit.

software license Contract signed by the purchaser of a software product in which he/she is usually made to agree not to make copies of the software for resale.

software package A prewritten program that can be purchased for use with a specific computer to perform a specific task. Usually includes the programs, stored on a storage media (floppy disk, CD-ROM and so on), and an operating manual.

software piracy The illegal copying and distribution of copyrighted software. See *piracy*.

software portability Ease with which a program can be moved from one computer environment to another. As third-party software becomes more prevalent in the computer industry, portability becomes a more valuable attribute of that software.

software publisher Business that designs, develops, and distributes software packages.

software upgrade A new, enhanced version of a developer's software. It usually contains features and functions not found in the earlier release.

sort To arrange data into a new sequence according to a logical system.

source code The language in which a program is written by the programmer. Symbolic coding in its original form before being processed by a computer. The computer automatically translates source code into a code the computer can understand.

source document A paper containing information that is to be input into the computer.

source program A program as originally coded, before being translated into machine language. It is converted to a machine language program by a *compiler, interpreter,* or *assembler.*

```
100    REM *** ODD OR EVEN ***
110    REM *** N - NUMBER ***
120    INPUT "TYPE THE NUMBER"; N
130    IF N = 0 THEN 220
140    REM *** CHECK FOR ODD OR EVEN ***
150    LET X = INT (N/2)
160    LET Y = N/2
170    IF X = Y THEN 200
180    PRINT N;"IS AN ODD NUMBER"
190    GOTO 120
200    PRINT N;"IS AN EVEN NUMBER"
210    GOTO 120
220    END
```

source program

spaghetti code An expression used to describe any badly designed and poorly structured program that is hard to understand. It often implies an excessive use of the GOTO statement. The term was first used by *Edsger Dijkstra.*

speech synthesis The computer generation of sound that resembles human speech. The synthesis is accomplished through the use of stored sounds and algorithms.

spelling checker Computer program, usually associated with word processing, that compares typed words against a word list and informs the user of possible spelling mistakes. A sophisticated spelling checker can have a base dictionary of well over 100,000 words and can provide the user with the ability to create special-purpose dictionaries of words not included in the base dictionary.

spline In computer graphics, a piecewise polynomial with at least first-order continuity between the pieces. A mathematically simple and elegant way to connect disjoint data points smoothly, hence, it is used not only for generating smooth curves and surfaces between sparse data points, but also for smooth motions between parameters sparsely located in time, such as those used to describe the key-frames in an animation.

spike A very short transient electrical signal, often of very high amplitude. See *power surge* and *surge protector.*

split screen Display screen that can be partitioned into two or more areas (windows) so different screen formats can be shown on the screen at the same time. It implies that one set of data can be manipulated independently of the other.

spreadsheet A software program that simulates a paper spreadsheet or worksheet, in which columns of numbers are summed for budgets and plans. A spreadsheet appears on screen as a matrix of rows and columns in which each intersection is defined as a cell.

	A	B	C	D	E	F	G	H	I
		Rent	Heat	Elec	Phone	Income1	Income2		Total
1									
2	Jan	385 00	75 00	65 00	75 00	1500 00	2200 00		3700 00
3	Feb	385 00	75 00	75 00	84 00	1500 00	2200 00		3700 00
4	Mar	385 00	75 00	57 00	65 00	1500 00	2200 00		3700 00
5	Apr	385 00	0 00	65 00	32 00	1500 00	2200 00		3700 00
6	May	385 00	0 00	70 00	84 00	1500 00	2200 00		3700 00
7	Jun	385 00	0 00	65 00	95 00	1500 00	2200 00		3700 00
8	Jul	385 00	0 00	72 00	87 00	1500 00	2200 00		3700 00
9	Aug	425 00	0 00	56 00	54 00	1500 00	2200 00		3700 00
10	Sept	425 00	50 00	87 00	54 00	1500 00	2700 00		4200 00
11	Oct	425 00	75 00	65 00	54 00	1500 00	2700 00		4200 00
12	Nov	425 00	125 00	89 00	84 00	1500 00	2700 00		4200 00
13	Dec	425 00	130 00	65 00	54 00	1500 00	2700 00		4200 00
14									
15	Total	4820 00	605 00	831 00	822 00	18000 00	28400 00		46400 00
16	Avg	771 25	94 58	133 08	130 75	2875 00	4550 00		7425 00
17	Max	425 00	130 00	89 00	95 00	1500 00	2700 00		4200 00
18									

Budget (SS)

spreadsheet

SSI See *small-scale integration*.

stack (1) Sequential data list stored in internal storage. Rather than addressing the stack elements by their memory locations, the computer retrieves information from the stack by popping elements from the top or from the bottom. See *pop* and *push*. (2) In HyperCard, refers to a file containing one or more cards that share a common background. See *HyperCard*.

standalone computer

standalone computer (1) Self-contained computer system that can work independently, not connected to or under the control of another computer system. A standalone system contains all the hardware and software a user requires. (2) Not connected to a network, or operating as if not connected to a network.

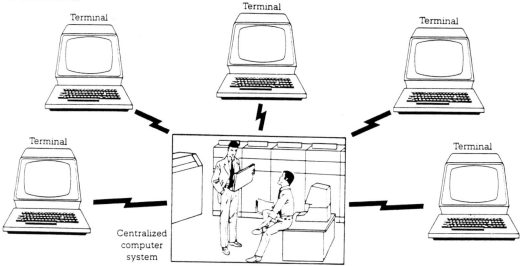

star network

star network One of the three principal topologies for a local area network, in which all computers and devices, known as nodes, are connected to one central computer, known as the hub. All communication between nodes is routed by the hub. See *bus network, network,* and *ring network*.

startup disk Diskette that contains the information to start the computer system.

startup screen A graphics file that, when placed in the System Folder on an Apple Macintosh computer, is displayed when the computer is turned on. Any bit-mapped graphic image can be used as a startup screen. For example, you can display a fish, a tree, or even a picture of a favorite movie star.

startup screen

state-of-the-art Having the most current hardware and software design and development.

status line A line of an application program's display screen that describes the state of the program.

Stibitz, George R. (1904-1995) Developed the Complex Calculator, one of the earliest forms of the digital computer (it was later called the Model I relay computer). The machine, first to use excess-three code and binary components, became an actual functioning device when Teletype machines were attached as input devices. At Dartmouth College, the capital of time-sharing systems, the first public demonstration of remote computer operation was staged in 1940 using the Complex Calculator. Stibitz built four more models of his computer. Today's computers can trace their roots back to Stibitz' talent and imagination. His binary computer, U.S. Patent No. 2,668,661 was issued in 1939.

George Stibitz

205

stickup initial In desktop publishing, an enlarged initial letter at the beginning of a paragraph that rises above the top of the first line.

storage Descriptive of a device or medium that can accept data, hold it, and deliver it on demand at a later time. The term is preferred over memory.

storage fragmentation A condition in which there are many scattered areas of storage that are too small to be used productively.

streaming cartridge A high-speed tape backup system, often used to make a complete backup of an entire hard disk.

street price The current price of a computer product at a computer store, mail order business, or other retail business. The street price of a product is often considerably lower than the retail price of a product. It is an average price charged by dealers around the country.

string Connected sequence of characters or bits treated as a single data item. The word "windsurfer" is a string of ten characters.

structured programming A programming technique used in the design and coding of computer programs. The approach assumes the disciplined use of a few basic coding structures and the use of top-down concepts to decompose main functions into lower-level components for modular coding purposes. The technique is concerned with improving the programming process through better organization and programs, and with better programming notation to facilitate correct and clear descriptions of data and control structures.

structured programming language A programming language that facilitates structured programming or top-down programming.

style sheet In word processing and desktop publishing, a file that contains formatting instructions but not text. Style sheets contain such information as margin sizes, column widths, paragraph indention, spacing, fonts, size, and style. Applying a stylesheet to text automatically formats the text according to the stylesheet's specifications.

stylus In computer graphics, a pointer that you operate in conjunction with a graphics tablet. To draw a point, the user touches the stylus (also called a pen) tip to the surface of the graphics tablet. The stylus and graphics tablet are preferred drawing devices for artists.

stylus

subdirectory File that lists the names of other files, and is displayed in a disk directory. This system allows files to be classified together to save space in a disk directory. A directory within another directory.

submenu An additional set of options related to a prior menu selection.

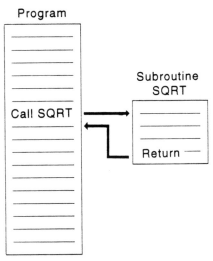

subroutine

subroutine Subsidiary routine within which initial execution never starts. Executed when called by some other program, usually the main program. Also called subprogram.

subscript (1) Integer value, appended to a variable name, that defines the storage elements composing an array or a matrix. (2) In noncomputer typefonts, a letter or digit written below and to the right of a symbol to distinguish it from variations of the same symbol. Contrast with *superscript*.

Sun Microsystems, Inc. A manufacturer of network-based, high-performance workstations founded in 1982.

supercomputer Largest, fastest, and most expensive mainframe computer available. Used by businesses and organizations that require extraordinary amounts of computing power. Sometimes called number crunchers because they perform between hundreds of millions to several billions of operations per second. They are very expensive and are typically used for the most complex computational tasks. Some applications of supercomputers include nuclear energy research, petroleum exploration, electronic design, realtime animated graphics, structural analysis, weather forecasting, 3-D seismic processing and oil field reservoir engineering.

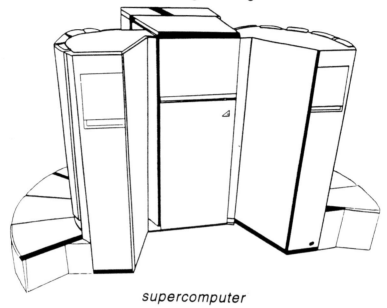

supercomputer

SuperPaint A popular graphics program that combines drawing and painting capabilities.

superscript Letter or digit written above and to the right of a symbol to denote a power or to identify a particular element of a set. Contrast with *subscript*.

Super VGA High-resolution video display standard for IBM microcomputers and compatibles.

support The assistance provided by a hardware or software vendor in installing, maintaining and learning their product.

surge A sudden and often destructive increase in line voltage. See *spike*.

surge protector Device that protects electrical equipment from being damaged by short surges of high voltage by filtering them out. A computer or other device is plugged into the surge protector, which itself is plugged into a standard electrical outlet. Also called surge suppressor.

synaptic microprocessor Federico Faggin presented the first chip endowed with a snyaptic internal logic system — that is, one mimicking the function of the human brain — in 1991. This synaptics I 1000, intended for OCR (Optical Character Recognition), was able to read up to 20,000 characters per second without error.

syntax The rules of a language. All programming languages have a syntax.

syntax error In a computer program, an error in the syntax, or vocabulary of a program.

syntax error

system A group of related components that interact to perform a task. A computer system is made up of the CPU, operating system, software, and peripheral devices.

system architecture The method or style in which a computer system is built.

system board See *motherboard*.

system disk The disk that contains the operating system and other systems programs that are necessary to start the computer.

system folder In an Apple Macintosh environment, the folder that contains the System File and the Finder, the two components of the Macintosh's operating system.

system operator (SYSOP) A person who manages an electronic bulletin board.

system programmer (1) Programmer who plans, generates, maintains, and controls the use of an operating system with the aim of improving the overall productivity of an installation. (2) Programmer who designs programming systems. Contrast with *application programmer.*

system prompt In an operating system such as DOS, the prompt that indicates the operating system's availability for entering commands.

system software Programs that run the computer system and aid the applications programmer in doing his/her task.

systems analysis and design The process of developing a system design to meet a new need or to solve a problem in an existing system.

System 7 Operating system for the Apple Macintosh computer. System 7 expands the Macintosh capabilities including an upgraded finder, file sharing capability, truetype fonts, inter-application communications and virtual memory.

systems analyst A person who performs systems analysis and design.

systems house An organization that develops customized software and/or turnkey systems for customers.

System/360 A series of mainframes introduced by the IBM Corporation in 1964. It was the first family of compatible computer systems ever introduced. The introduction of this family of computers brought about the third generation of computers.

System/370 A mainframe product line introduced by the IBM Corporation in 1970. This product line replaced the System/360 family of computers.

System/390 A mainframe product line introduced by the IBM Corporation in 1990 to supersede the System/370 family of computers.

tab Carriage control that specifies output columns.

table Collection of data in a form suitable for ready reference. The data are frequently stored in consecutive storage locations or written in the form of an array of rows and columns for easy entry. An intersection of labeled rows and columns serves to locate a specific piece of information. Tables are useful for holding tabular data, like the data found in spreadsheets.

tactile screen In 1985 Zenith presented the first tactile screen system, based on surface acoustic wave technology; all the user has to do to give a command is touch a section of the screen.

tagged image file format (TIFF) A common file format used to store bit-mapped graphic images. TIFF simulates gray-scale shading.

Tandy Corporation A leading manufacturer of personal computer and electronics. In 1977, Tandy introduced one of the first personal computers, the Radio Shack TRS-80 Model I. Several other TRS-80 models were developed, and in 1984, Tandy started building IBM-compatible microcomputers. Today, Tandy markets a varie of microcomputer systems through their company-owned Radio Shack stores.

tape Strip of material that may be coated with a magnetically sensitive substance and used for data input, storage, or output. Data are usually stored serially in several channels across the tape, transversely to the reading or writing motion.

tape backup A device that uses magnetic tape to back up files.

target (1) The desired destination. (2) The place to which information is supposed to be copied. (3) Something that is being searched for.

tear-off menu A screen menu that can be moved off its primary position, relocated to any part of the display screen and kept active.

technical support Technical advise provided to registered users of a hardware device or program. Many computer companies offer technical support for the products they manufacture.

telecommunications Transfer of data from one place to another over long distances, using telephone lines, microwaves and/or satellites.

telecommuting Working at home with telecommunications between office and home.

template (1) Plastic guide used in drawing geometric flowcharting symbols. (2) In computer graphics, the pattern of a standard, commonly used component or part that serves as a design aid. Once created, it can be subsequently traced instead of redrawn whenever needed. (3) In a spreadsheet program, a worksheet that has already been designed for the solution of a specific type of problem. (4) Plastic sheet placed over keyboard keys to help the user remember tasks performed by each key. (5) In page layout and word processing programs, templates are predesigned page formats. You use the template by loading the file, adding the text and/or graphic images, and printing.

tera Prefix indicating one trillion.

terabyte One trillion or 1,099,511,627,776 bytes or characters. It is abbreviated TB.

terminal

terminal An input/output device for a computer that usually has a keyboard for input and video screen for output.

terminator A device attached to the last peripheral in a series, or the last node on a network.

testing   Involves running a program with sample data, in order to debug it.

text   Words, sentences, paragraphs, and numbers that express the information to be conveyed.

text editing   General term that covers any additions, changes, or deletions made to electronically stored material.

text editor   Computer program used to manipulate text; for example, to erase, insert, change, and move words or groups of words. The manipulated text may be another computer program.

text file   File containing information expressed in text form. Same as *data file*.

texture   In computer graphics, any 2-D pattern used to add the appearance of complexity to a 3-D surface without actually modeling the complexity. For example, a surface could be made to appear reflective to simulate glass or metal, or a brick texture pattern could be used on an architectural drawing of a brick house.

texture

text wrap   A feature supported by some word processing and desktop publishing programs that allows you to contour type around a graphic.

thermal wax-transfer printer   A nonimpact printer. A nonimpact printer that uses heat to melt colored wax onto paper to create an image. It uses pins to apply the heat.

third generation computers Computers that use integrated circuitry and miniaturization of components to replace transistors, reduce costs, work faster, and increase reliability. Introduced in 1964 and still the primary technology for digital computers.

third-party vendor A firm that markets an accessory hardware or software product for a given brand of computer equipment.

Thomas, Charles Xavier Made a calculating machine in 1820 credited with being the first that ever did work practically and usefully. This machine, which was widely sold, contained units for setting, counting, and registering. It has a driving wheel with nine rows of teeth side by side, the rows having from one to nine teeth each. A movable recording wheel is engaged with one of these rows, and is advanced according to the number of teeth in the row. In Europe, Arthur Burkhardt began manufacturing in 1878, a Thomas type of machine known as the Arithmometer.

Charles Thomas

Thompson, Kenneth A Bell Laboratories research scientist who, in 1971, with Dennis Ritchie, developed and implemented the UNIX operating system. The UNIX system has led a generation of software designers to new ways of thinking about programming. His research has centered around compiler technology, programming languages, and operating systems. He developed an algorithm for playing chess. One of his chess playing programs, BELLE, won the world computer chess championship.

Kenneth Thompson

three-dimensional graphics (3-D) A graphic image in three dimensions — height, width and depth. A three-dimensional image is rendered on a two-dimensional medium; the third dimension, depth, is usually indicated by shading or by means of perspective.

three-dimensional spreadsheet A program that allows two or more spreadsheets to be linked together and incorporated into another spreadsheet.

throughput The speed with which a computer can process data.

thumbnail In desktop publishing, a small image showing the preliminary layout of a page.

TIFF An acronym for Tagged Image File Format, a standard format for recording bit-mapped images on disk. TIFF files can store images of any size with any number of colors, using several kinds of data compression.

tiled windows A method of dividing the display screen into sections without overlapping one another.

timed backup A program feature that saves the file you are working on at specified intervals, such as every five minutes.

time-sharing Method of operation in which a computer facility is shared by several users for different purposes at (apparently) the same time. Although the computer actually services each user in sequence, the high speed of the computer makes it appear as though the users are all handled simultaneously.

title bar In a graphics environment, the line of text at the top of a window that indicates the name of the application or file in that window.

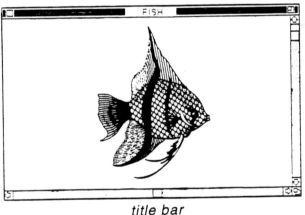

title bar

toggle (1) A keystroke that turns a function of a program on or off. (2) A device having two stable states. (3) The ability to go back and forth between two distinctly separate functions on a CRT.

token A special type of packet used to arbitrate data communications.

token-ring network A type of local area network in which permission to transmit over the network is contained in a special message called a token (special bit configuration).

toner cartridge In a laser printer, the disposable container that holds the electrically charged dry ink (and sometimes a drum) used in creating an image on the paper. The dry ink (toner) is fused to paper in laser printing.

tool (1) An object or icon used to perform operations in a computer program. Tools are often named either by what they do or by the type of object on which they work. (2) In some computer systems, an applications program. (3) In artificial intelligence, an inference engine, a user interface, and procedures for entering knowledge.

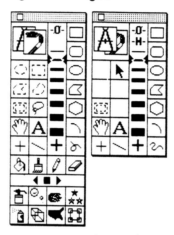

tool

toolbox (1) A set of standard routines (pointing, cropping, drawing, etc.) provided by a program or operating system that can be called on by other programs or by the user. (2) An on-screen group of icons representing these routines.

top-down design An approach to writing a structured program in which the program is divided into blocks or modules that are written individually and then combined into the final program.

topology The geometric arrangement in which the nodes of a local area network are connected to each other, usually a bus, ring, or star configuration. See *network*.

touch-sensitive screen Display screen on which the user can enter commands by pressing designated areas with a finger or other object. This method takes advantage of an individual's natural instinct to point.

tower configuration A cabinet for a personal computer that is designed to stand upright on the floor with components stacked on top of each other. Tower cases usually have much more room for accessories.

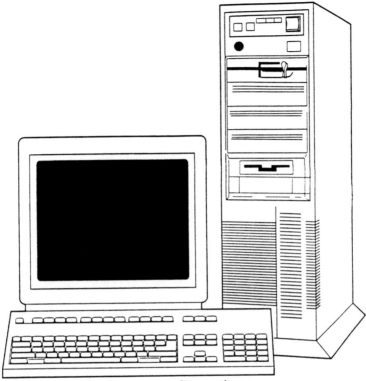

tower configuration

track (1) Path along which data are recorded on a continuous or rotational medium, such as magnetic tape or magnetic disk. (2) To follow or record the moving position of a video display cursor, stylus, mouse, or other input device.

trackball Device used to move the cursor around on a computer display screen. Consists of a mounting, usually a box, in which is set a ball. As the user spins the ball, the cursor moves at the speed and in the direction of the ball's motion. The housing is stationary, as opposed to the mobile mouse unit.

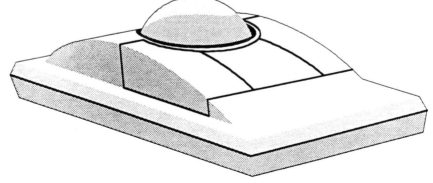

trackball

tracking Moving a cursor or predefined symbol across the surface of the visual display screen with a light pen, electronic pen, trackball, or mouse.

tracking

tractor-feed mechanism Pair of pin-studded belts that rotate in unison and pull paper, punched with marginal holes, into a printer.

traffic The volume of messages sent over a data communications line.

transfer (1) To copy or read, transmit, and store an item or block of information. (2) To change control.

transistor A switch-like electronic device that lets electrical current pass through only if a specific charge is applied to it.

translate To change data from one form of representation to another without significantly affecting the meaning.

translator A program that translates a program written in a high-level programming language into its object code, the form in which the computer can understand. Assemblers, compilers, and interpreters are all translators.

transmission Sending of data from one location and receiving of data in another location, usually leaving the source data unchanged.

transparent Refers to something the equipment does that the user is not aware of.

trapdoor An undocumented entry point into an otherwise secure system. During software development, programmers often create entry points into "their" programs to aid in debugging and adding final enhancements. These trapdoors are supposed to be closed or removed before the program goes through the promotion to production process. Many times, however, they are not. This breach leaves an unadvertised but very real hole in the system's security.

tree structure A way of organizing information into a hierarchical structure with a root and branches; a form of database organization.

trigger Button on a joystick.

Trojan horse Pertaining to a crime in which a computer criminal places instructions in someone else's program that will allow the program to function normally but also to perform illegitimate functions.

troubleshooting Trying to find a malfunction in a hardware unit or a mistake in a computer program. Synonymous with *debug*.

True BASIC Structured version of the BASIC programming language. Developed in 1983 by the inventors of the original BASIC language, John Kemeny and Thomas Kurtz. True BASIC is a version of BASIC that does not require line numbers and that includes advanced control structures that make structured programming possible. See *Kemeny, John* and *Kurtz, Thomas*.

```
REM   Perfect numbers

LIBRARY "numlib.trc"
DECLARE DEF sum_div

LET t1 = time          ! Time it
FOR n = 1 to 10000
    CALL factor(n)
    CALL prime_powers
    IF sum_div = 2*n then PRINT n
NEXT n
LET t2 = time
PRINT round(t2-t1,2); "secs."

END
```
True BASIC program

TrueType A trademark for a high-level outline font technology developed by Apple Computer. TrueType provides scalable fonts to both the display screen and the printer.

truncate (1) To cut off the final digits in a number, thus lessening precision; for example, 3.14159 truncates the series for π, which could conceivably be extended indefinitely. (2) To cut off any characters that will not fit into an allotted space.

```
program ArithmeticMean;
var
    Num1, Num2, Num3, Average       :Real;
begin
    Num1 := 31.0;
    Num2 := 84.0;
    Num3 := 26.0;
    Average := (Num1 + Num2 + Num3) / 3;
    WriteLn('The average is ', Average:6:1)
end.
```

Turbo Pascal program

Turbo Pascal A very popular variation of the Pascal programming language. Turbo Pascal provides an integrated package that includes an editor, compiler and linker. Turbo Pascal was designed in 1984 by Philippe Kahn of Borland International, and closely follows the definition of standard Pascal. In addition to the standard, Turbo Pascal includes a number of extensions to the language.

Turing, Alan M. (1912-1954) English mathematician and logician who, shortly before his death, completed the design of one of the world's first modern high-speed digital computers (Colossus). Acknowledged by many as the father of artificial intelligence. He argued that a machine could be built which could emulate human thinking. In 1937, Turing published a famous paper in which he envisioned an abstract computing machine called the Turing machine, which could be fed instructions from paper tape. In recognition of his outstanding pioneering work, the Association for Computing Machinery has named its most prestigious award, The Turing Award. It is awarded annually for contributions to computer science of a technical nature.

Alan Turing

turnaround time The time it takes for a vendor to respond to your request for support or maintenance.

turnkey system

turnkey system Prepackaged, ready-to-use computer system containing all the hardware, software, training, and maintenance support needed to perform a given application. All the prepared system needs is the "turn of the key." For example, a turnkey desktop publishing system might consist of a CPU, monitor, hard disk, scanner, laser printer and appropriate software. While easier to set up than off-the-shelf systems, equipment, training, and support choices are sometimes limited.

turtle graphics A graphics system first developed for the LOGO language. It consists of a turtle, which is displayed on the graphics screen and can be pointed and moved by simple commands. A variation of turtle graphics has been found to be useful for generating fractal curves. See *LOGO*.

tutorial An instructional book or program that takes the user through a prescribed sequence of steps in order to learn a product.

TWAIN A cross-platform, interapplication interface standard that lets you use a scanner with any TWAIN-compatible application (such as Photoshop) rather than having to use an application dedicated to that particular scanner.

twisted-pair cable A cable containing one or more pairs of intertwined wires.

typeface Collection of letters, numbers, and symbols that share a distinctive appearance. (e.g. Helvetica, Times Roman, Bodoni, Schoolbook, Courier, and Palatino).

typeface family A group of typefaces that include the normal, bold, italic and bold-italic variations of the same design; a related group of type fonts.

typesetting The production of camera-ready copy on a laser printer (low-quality typesetting) or an imagesetter (high-quality typesetting).

type style The weight (such as normal or bold) or posture (such as italic) of a font.

ULSI See *ultra large-scale integration*.

ultra large-scale integration (ULSI) Process of placing millions of electronic components on a single chip. See *integrated circuit*.

unbundled software Pertaining to services, programs, training, and so on sold independently of computer hardware by the hardware manufacturer. Contrast with *bundled*.

undelete A program feature that can restore a file that was accidentally erased from disk.

undo Command that undoes the effect of the previous command and puts the text or graphics back the way it was. Some programs provide multiple undo levels, letting you take back commands you gave in the past.

Unisys A computer company formed in 1986 as a merger of the Burroughs Corporation and Sperry Corporation, both large mainframe manufacturers. Unisys continues to emphasize the product lines of both companies, and in addition has introduced several new mainframe, minicomputer, and personal computer products.

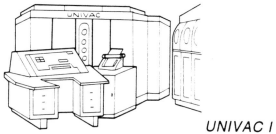

UNIVAC I

UNIVAC I First commercial electronic digital computer. Completed in 1951, it was used by the Census Bureau for processing some of the data from the 1950 census. Forty-eight of these computers were built.

UNIX An easy-to-use operating system developed by Ken Thompson, Dennis Ritchie and coworkers at Bell Laboratories. Since the UNIX operating system is very easy to use, its design concept had a great influence on operating systems for microcomputers. UNIX is widely used on a great variety of computers, from mainframes to microcomputers.

unjustified text Text as it appears when typed on the display screen. It is not centered or justified.

UPC Acronym for Universal Product Code. It is a machine-readable code of parallel bars used for labeling products in retail store automation systems.

UPC

update To modify a graphics file and make it reflect more recent information.

upgrade (1) To apply an enhancement or other improvement to a hardware or software component of an existing system. (2) To replace a software program with a more recently released version or a hardware device with one that provides better performance.

upload To transfer information (files) from a smaller computer to a larger computer.

upward compatible Term used to indicate that a computer system or peripheral device can do everything that the previous model could do, plus some additional functions. See *compatibility*.

USENET A worldwide, public-access network on the Internet used for electronic mail and special interest groups. It is the mother of all electronic bulletin boards and is accessed by over 15 million people in more than 100 countries.

user Any person authorized to operate any aspect of a computer system.

user-friendly Term applied to software and/or hardware that has been designed to be easily used, without the user having to remember complex procedures. Very easy for the inexperienced person to use.

user group Group of computer users who share the knowledge they have gained and the programs they have developed on a computer or class of computers of a specific manufacturer. Usually meet to exchange information, share programs, and trade equipment.

user group

user interface The features of a program or computer that govern the way it communicates with the person who is using it.

utility programs Computer programs that provide commonly needed services, such as performing mathematical functions or transferring data from one medium to another.

vaccine An application program designed to counter the effects of a virus program.

value (1) Any constant or quantity stored in a computer's memory. (2) In a spreadsheet, data consisting of a number representing an amount, a formula, or a function. (3) In computer graphics, the character of color or tone assessed on a scale from dark to light.

vaporware Slang for announced software that may never materialize. In other words, a program promised by a publisher but never released.

variable Quantity that can assume any of a given set of values. For example, in a BASIC program that states PRINT A, B, C, the variables A, B, and C represent the actual values that will be printed. Contrast with *constant*.

VDT Acronym for Video Display Terminal, an input/output device consisting of a display screen and an input keyboard.

vector (1) List of numbers, all of which are expressed on the same line, such as a single column or row. (2) Quantity having magnitude and direction, as opposed to scaler value. (3) In computer science, a data structure that permits the location of any item by the use of a single index or subscript. (4) Type of cathode ray tube on which graphic data are represented by lines drawn from point to point rather than by illumination of a series of contiguous positions, as on a raster display device. (5) In plotting, an element of a line connecting two points. (6) In computer graphics, a line drawn in a certain direction from a starting point to an ending point. See *object-oriented graphics*.

vector graphics See *object-oriented graphics*.

vendor Anyone who sells services or supports computer products for profit.

Ventura Publisher A desktop publishing program for IBM PC, IBM PS/2 and Apple Macintosh computers from Ventura Software, Inc. The program provides typeset-quality desktop publishing.

verify (1) To determine whether a data processing operation has been accomplished accurately. (2) To check data validity.

version Specific release of a software product of a specific hardware model. Usually numbered in ascending order. For example, DOS 6.0 is a later version of a disk operating system than is DOS 5.0 or DOS 4.1.

vertical software Software designed for a unique use. For example, a restaurant has needs different from a sunglass distributor, so the restaurant would purchase vertical software for its type of business.

very large-scale integration (VLSI) Process of placing between 100,000-1,000,000 electronic components on a single chip. See *integrated circuit.*

VGA Acronym for Video Graphics Array. An IBM high-resolution video display standard for its personal computers. VGA displays images at 640 pixels horizontally by 480 pixels vertically. This color bit-mapped graphics display standard was introduced by IBM Corporation in 1987 with its Personal System/2 computer.

VHSIC An acronym for Very High-Speed Integrated Circuit, an integrated circuit that performs operations, usually logic operations, at a very high rate of speed. The higher the speed of logic circuits, the greater the amount of information can be processed in a specific amount of time.

video adapter A plug-in circuit board that generates the output required to display computer text and graphics on a monitor.

videodisk An optical disk used for the storage and retrieval of still pictures or television pictures and sound. A videodisk player, which can be controlled by a computer, is used to play back the videodisk on a standard television monitor.

video display terminal (VDT) Device for entering information into a computer system and displaying information on a screen. A typewriterlike keyboard is used to enter information.

video display terminal (VDT)

view (1) To display information on a computer display screen. (2) The display of a graphical image from a given perspective. (3) In CAD programs, an image of a 3-D graphics model as it would be seen from a particular viewpoint. (4) In database systems, way of presenting the contents of a database to the user, not necessarily the same as the way the fields and records are stored in the database.

virtual memory Storage that is actually provided on a disk drive or other mass storage device but appears to programs to be part of the main memory of the computer. Thus, the programs seem to use more main memory that is actually provided.

virtual reality A system that simulates real life or reality. Virtual reality exploits sophisticated, multi-dimensional imaging systems and high-speed processing capabilities, creating environments with which users can interact and manipulate directly. With such simulated systems you can fly a jet airplane, travel through space, and walk on a circus high-wire, all without ever getting your feet off the ground. Equipment used in virtual reality systems include special goggles, helmet with speakers, power gloves, sound board, and vibrating platforms. Pilots train on the ground with virtual reality systems that imitate flight conditions and respond to their input as an actual airplane might.

virus A computer program which can wreak havoc on a system, either by destroying data or simply gumming up the works. It is called a virus because it acts like a biological virus does in a human — the computer virus is not actually a live organism. Viruses usually enter via shareware or public domain programs, though there have been reports of viruses being carried by commercial software.

Visual BASIC A dialect of the BASIC programming language developed by Microsoft Corporation for Windows.

VLSI See *very large-scale integration.*

voice mail Messages spoken into a telephone, converted into digital form, and stored in the computer's memory until recalled, at which time they are reconverted into voice form.

voice output Computer output in the form of synthesized speech.

voice recognition system System designed to recognize and understand the voice and vocabulary of the user.

voice synthesis See *speech synthesis.*

volatile storage A device which requires continuous electrical power to keep from losing information RAM storage is a volatile storage.

von Neumann, John (1903-1957) One of the outstanding mathematicians of this century. He was the genius behind the stored program computer. von Neumann made important contributions to the foundations of mathematics, logic, quantum physics, computers, and game theory. He published a paper in 1946 that became the definitive paper in the computer field. The work delineated the design of a stored program computer, and von Neumann anticipated problems by proposing ingenious solutions. He was also a consultant on the atomic bomb project in 1943.

John von Neumann

wait state An amount of time spent waiting for some operation to take place.

wand A device for reading labels on retail goods in a point-of-sale automation system.

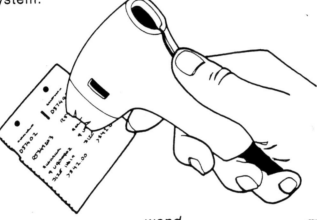

wand

Wang, An (1920-1990) Came from China to the U.S. in 1945 to study applied physics at Harvard University. In 1951 he found Wang Laboratories, Inc., a computer manufacturing company he guided for almost 40 years. In 1988, two years before he died, Wang was inducted into the National Inventors' Hall of Fame for his 1948 invention of a pulse transfer device that enabled magnetic core memories to be used in computers. He sold his patent for this key process to the IBM Corporation for the bargain basement price of $400,000. He used the proceeds to set up Wang Laboratories over a Boston garage.

An Wang

warm boot See *bootstrapping.*

Watson, Thomas J., Jr. (1914-1993) Son of Thomas Watson, Sr., founder of the IBM Corporation. Thomas Watson, Jr. joined IBM in 1937. In 1956, Watson, Sr. handed over control of IBM to his older son, who guided the company into its leadership position in the computer industry. He pursued the idea that IBM had to develop a computer that would perform impressively in those areas where computers were most in demand — science and defense. The fruit of those efforts was the IBM 701 computer. Dramatic improvements in computer speed and versatility occurred in the 1950s. In 1964, IBM announced a new computer, System/360, capable of handling both business and scientific applications. Watson, Jr. retired from IBM in 1974. See *IBM Corporation.*

Thomas Watson, Jr.

Watson, Thomas J., Sr. (1874-1956) Guiding spirit of IBM Corporation, a superb salesman and president of IBM until 1956. Although his motto was THINK, he did not think there would be much demand for digital computers. Watson, Sr. was responsible for instilling a strict professional demeanor in his employees that set IBMers apart from employees of competitive computer companies. The IBM Corporation has influenced our modern information processing era like no other company. Watson created a corporate culture, an esprit de corps that is the envy of the business world to this day. In 1914, Watson, Sr. took over a demoralized little collection of 13 companies and welded them into a single entity that dominated the market for card equipment, and grew into the world's largest computer company. See *IBM Corporation.*

Thomas Watson, Sr.

weight The variation in the heaviness of a typeface.

what if? (1) Premise on which most electronic spreadsheet programs operate. New values may be substituted to determine the resultant effect on other values. (2) In artificial intelligence, a term used in expert systems. The process is as follows: once a set of data have been entered, questions have been answered, and a conclusion has been reached, changing a portion of the data of answering a question differently to see how the conclusion would be altered.

wide area network (WAN) Data communications network designed to serve an area of hundreds or thousands of miles. WAN's are generally implemented by linking together several remote Local Area Networks (LANs) through the use of gateways and bridges over dedicated telephone lines, satellite dishes or radio waves. See *local area network*.

widow Last line of a paragraph sitting alone at the top of a page of text. Considered undesirable in all forms of printing. Compare with *orphan*.

Wiener, Norbert (1894-1964) One of the most brilliant mathematicians that the United States ever produced, is best known for establishing the science of cybernetics, which is concerned with the common factors of control and communication in living organisms, automatic machines, and organizations, especially the mathematical analysis of the flow of information in such systems. In 1919 he joined the faculty of the Massachusetts Institute of Technology. Wiener was also very conscious of the long-range impact of the computer on man and society. In a 1950 publication he warned of the dangers that could be caused by selfish exploitation of the computer's potential.

Norbert Wiener

wildcard Method of file-naming conventions that permits an operating system to perform utility functions on multiple files with related names, without the programmer or user having to specify each file by its full, unique name.

Wilkes, Maurice Vincent (born 1913) A British computer pioneer that became director of the Mathematics Laboratory at Cambridge University after World War II. In 1949, his computer technology development team completed the Electronic Delayed Storage Automatic Computer (EDSAC), which stored 512 words of 34 bits each. The EDSAC, which boasted 3000 electronic valves, could add two numbers in 70 microseconds, multiplying them in 8.5 milliseconds. But where the mighty machine really scored was in its storage — both programs and data could be contained in the same store, which allowed greater flexibility in programming. In 1957, Wiles went on to become the first president of the British Computer Society.

Maurice Wilkes

window Portion of the video display area dedicated to some specific purpose. Special software allows the screen to be divided into multiple windows that can be moved around and made bigger or smaller. Windows allow the user to treat the computer display screen like a desktop where various files can remain open simultaneously.

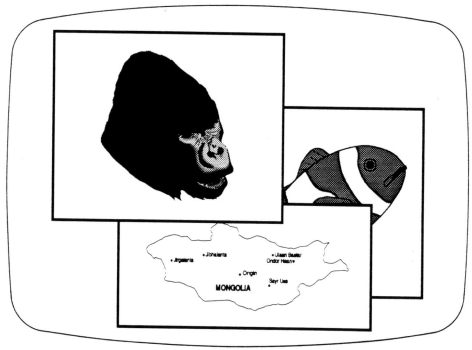

window

windowing software Programs that enable users to work with multiple on-screen windows. The Apple Macintosh Finder, Microsoft Windows and the OS/2 Presentation Manager are all examples of windowing environments.

Windows A graphics-based operating environment for IBM-compatible microcomputers from Microsoft Corporation. It runs in conjunction with DOS. Some of the graphical user interface features include pull-down menus, multiple typefaces, desk accessories, and the capability of moving text and graphics from one program to another via a clipboard.

Windows 95 A popular version of Microsoft Windows released in 1995. Windows 95 provides for 32-bit data input/output, better graphics performance, and better overall performance for high-end personal computers.

Wirth, Niklaus In 1968, in Switzerland, he developed the computer language Pascal (named for Blaise Pascal), a popular high-level programming language that facilitates the use of structured programming techniques. In 1979, Wirth created Modula-2, an enhanced version of Pascal that supports the separate compilation of program modules and overcomes many other shortcomings of Pascal.

Niklaus Wirth

word A group of bytes that occupies one location in the computer's storage.

Word See *Microsoft Word*.

word length The number of bits in a computer word.

WordPerfect A popular, fully featured word processor introduced by WordPerfect Corporation in 1980.

WordPerfect Corporation A software corporation founded in 1980. The company is best known for their flagship product, WordPerfect, a full-featured word processing program.

word processing (WP) Technique for electronically storing, editing, and manipulating text by using an electronic keyboard, computer, and printer. The text is recorded on a magnetic medium, usually floppy disks. The final

233

output is on paper. Words and letters are manipulated electronically, making it easy to copy and edit text.

WordStar A popular, full-featured word processing program introduced by WordStar International in 1978. It is available on IBM-compatible computers.

word wrap Feature that automatically moves a word to the beginning of the next line if it will not fit at the end of the original line. Feature found in word processing and page layout programs.

Works See *Microsoft Works*.

worksheet The document created and edited with a spreadsheet program. See *spreadsheet*.

workstation Configuration of computer equipment designed for use by one person at a time. This may have a terminal connected to a computer, or it may be a stand-alone system with local processing capability. Examples of workstations are a stand-alone graphics system, and a word processing system.

workstation

World-Wide Web (WWW) A system that enables you to access hypertest-based documents that have been linked across the Internet.

worm A program that scans a system or an entire network for available, unused disk space in which to run. Originally, worms were developed by systems programmers searching for fragments of memory in which to run segments of large programs. They tend to tie up all computing resources in a system or on a network and effectively shut it down.

WORM An acronym for Write Once, Read Many times, which refers to a type of optical disk where a computer can save information once, then read that information, but cannot change it.

Wozniak, Stephen (born 1950) Possibly the one person most responsible for putting the personal computer and his home turf of Silicon Valley on the industry map. The brilliant computer whiz, affectionately known as Woz, designed both the Apple I and Apple II microcomputers that launched the home computer industry. Wozniak teamed up with Steven Jobs in 1976 to form Apple Computer Inc., which has taken an incredible journey from garage shop to multibillion dollar concern in only a few years. Woz left Apple to obtain a computer science degree from the University of California, and to design a remote control home video device for his own corporation, CL-9 (Cloud-9). See *Apple Computer Inc.* and *Jobs, Steven.*

Stephen Wozniak

wraparound type Type that wraps around a graphic image in a body of text.

write (1) Process of transferring information from the computer to an output medium. (2) To record data in a storage device. Contrast with *read.*

write enable notch A rectangular hole cut into a 5.25-inch diskette, that is used to indicate to the drive that this diskette can be written to.

write-protected disk A diskette whose contents can be read by a disk drive but cannot be changed or erased.

write protect switch A switch built into a 3.5-inch floppy disk which lets the disk drive know whether it is okay to write to the disk.

wysiwyg An acronym for What You See Is What You Get, a popular description for computer systems that supposedly always display upon the screen an accurate replica of what will eventually be transferred to hard copy.

x-axis On a coordinate plane, the horizontal axis.

XENIX A version of UNIX, designed by Mircosoft Corporation, for use on IBM-compatible microcomputers.

x-height The height of lowercase letters without ascenders and descenders.

x-y plotter Output device that draws points, lines, or curves on a sheet of paper based on *x* and *y* coordinates from a computer.

x-y-z coordinate system A three-dimensional system of Cartesian coordinates that includes a third (*z*) axis running perpendicular to the horizontal (*x*) and vertical (*y*) axis.

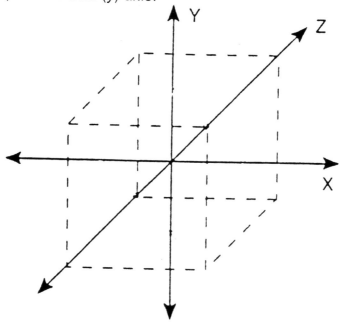

x-y-z coordinate system

y-axis On a coordinate plane, the vertical axis.

zap Erase, destroy or obliterate. Commonly used to describe deleting a file from disk storage.

z-axis On a coordinate plane, the axis that represents depth.

zooming Changing of a view on a graphics display by either moving in on successively smaller portions of the currently visible picture or moving out until the window encloses the entire scene. Capability that proportionally enlarges or reduces a figure displayed on a visual display screen.

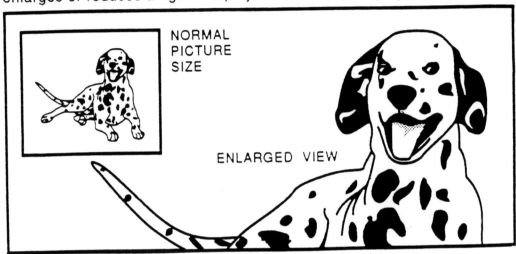

NORMAL PICTURE SIZE

ENLARGED VIEW

zooming

Zuse, Konrad A German engineer who started work on program controlled computing machines in the early 1930s and produced his first machine, the Z1, in 1938. In 1939 he was drafted into the German army. In his spare time, he created the electromechanical Z2. Another version, the Z3, completed in 1941, was a fully functional, program-controlled, general purpose electro-mechanical computer. Next came the more sophisticated Z4, which was the only Zuse Z machine to survive the war. After the war, Zuse developed Plankalkul, an early programming language. He formed his own computer manufacturing company, Zuse AG, which was eventually acquired by Siemens in 1969.

Konrad Zuse